MW01247701

GREATER IS **HE** **THAT** IS IN **YOU**, **THAN HE THAT** IS IN THE **WORLD**

GREATER IS HE THAT IS IN YOU, THAN HE THAT IS IN THE WORLD

Defining
Your Power
With The
Holy Spirit
Living Within
A Six Step
Workshop Series

MARGO ANN HOLLEY

XULON PRESS

Xulon Press
555 Winderley Pl, Suite 225
Maitland, FL 32751
407.339.4217
www.xulonpress.com

© 2024 by Margo Ann Holley

All rights reserved solely by the author. The author guarantees all contents
are original and do not infringe upon the legal rights of any other person
or work. No part of this book may be reproduced in any form without the
permission of the author.

Due to the changing nature of the Internet, if there are any web addresses,
links, or URLs included in this manuscript, these may have been altered and
may no longer be accessible. The views and opinions shared in this book belong
solely to the author and do not necessarily reflect those of the publisher. The
publisher therefore disclaims responsibility for the views or opinions
expressed within the work.

Unless otherwise indicated, Scripture quotations taken from the Holy Bible,
New Living Translation (NLT). Copyright ©1996, 2004, 2007 by Tyndale House
Foundation. Used by permission of Tyndale House Publishers, Inc.

Scripture quotations taken from the Holman Christian Standard Bible (HCSB).
Copyright © 1999, 2000, 2002, 2003, 2009 by Holman Bible Publishers,
Nashville Tennessee. All rights reserved.

Scripture quotations taken from the Holy Bible, New International Version
(NIV). Copyright © 1973, 1978, 1984, 2011 by Biblica, Inc.™. Used by
permission. All rights reserved.

Scripture quotations taken from the King James Version
(KJV)—*public domain.*

Paperback ISBN-13: 978-1-66289-325-4
eBook ISBN-13: 978-1-66289-326-1

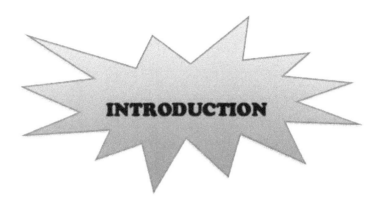

Introduction:

I HAVE CONSTRUCTED 6 workshops to help you truly understand that you are a Superhero in this world as a Christian. These workshops will help you define what God's mission is for your life and the life of others. You will understand that being a part of God's Gospel League as a Christian is about spreading His Word (the Good News) to help save the lost of the world. 1 John 4:4 proves that you are a Superhero as a Christian.

1 John 4:4 (NLT)

⁴ But you belong to God, my dear children. You have already won a victory over those people, because the Spirit who lives in you is greater than the spirit who lives in the world.

As Christians we must always hold to the truth (God's Word), live by it and apply it to our own life.

Through these workshops you will see that being a superhero for God is not about pleasing yourself (satisfying your own desires) – but to help save the lost of the world. This is the main mission for most Marvel Superheroes and God's mission for us as Christians.

These workshops will allow you to see:

- That a superhero never has time to allow anything to get in the way of completing God's mission. This works the same way as Christians. We can't allow anything other than God to become our idol such as: (a job, money, a sport or hobby, etc....). These things will get in the way of completing the mission that God has called us to complete. As the superhero works hard to complete their mission along with watching out for the enemy – he/she must be on constant alert to prevent taking a fall while trying to accomplish the mission. This is also true for Christians. As Christians we must live by *Ephesians 6:10-18*. *(see below)*.

Ephesians 6:10-18 (NLT)

[10]A final word: Be strong in the Lord and in his mighty power. [11]Put on all of God's armor so that you will be able to stand firm against all

strategies of the devil. [12] For we are not fighting against flesh-and-blood enemies, but against evil rulers and authorities of the unseen world, against mighty powers in this dark world, and against evil spirits in the heavenly places. [13] Therefore, put on every piece of God's armor so you will be able to resist the enemy in the time of evil. Then after the battle you will still be standing firm. [14] Stand your ground, putting on the belt of truth and the body armor of God's righteousness. [15] For shoes, put on the peace that comes from the Good News so that you will be fully prepared. [16] In addition to all of these, hold up the shield of faith to stop the fiery arrows of the devil. [17] Put on salvation as your helmet, and take the sword of the Spirit, which is the word of God. [18] Pray in the Spirit at all times and on every occasion. Stay alert and be persistent in your prayers for all believers everywhere.

- In these workshops you will also define what it is to be a mighty team working together. In the Book of Acts, chapters 14-16 it shows great examples of how the apostles worked together to spread God's Word. They stayed committed in spreading the Gospel, even if it meant that they had to die trying. In the Marvel Superhero World, Batman and Robin were great teammates that were able to accomplish each mission that they were set out to achieve. You will see that when a superhero chooses a teammate, his/her teammate should be on the same mission. This works the same way as a Christian. Your spiritual mate of choice should also be a mighty man/woman of God – so the two of you can work together on God's mission to help change the world – by winning the souls of the lost. Superman and Superwoman are also great examples of a mighty team. In the bible, Jonathan and King David were also great teammates. Jesus and his twelve disciples are another great example of great teammates. The bible states that we should be equally yoked (2 Corinthians 6:14) – see below.

2 Corinthians 6:14 (NLT)

[14] Don't team up with those who are unbelievers. How can righteousness be a partner with wickedness? How can light live with darkness?

Again, when a superhero is on a mission – there is always an enemy to fight – just as our lives as Christians. While carrying out God's mission, we must fight off our enemy, Satan and his mighty army (the temptations of sin through the struggles and challenges that we deal with each and every day). People can also put things in front of us to intimidate us to make us fall short.

Remember the story of Nehemiah when he was trying to rebuild the wall in Jerusalem for God, people were sent to him to try and intimidate him through getting God's work done. Read what it says here in Nehemiah in chapter 6 – verses: 1-9 (see below)

Nehemiah 6:1-9 (NLT)

¹Sanballat, Tobiah, Geshem the Arab, and the rest of our enemies found out that I had finished rebuilding the wall and that no gaps remained—though we had not yet set up the doors in the gates. ²So Sanballat and Geshem sent a message asking me to meet them at one of the villages in the plain of Ono. But I realized they were plotting to harm me, ³so I replied by sending this message to them: "I am engaged in a great work, so I can't come. Why should I stop working to come and meet with you?" ⁴Four times they sent the same message, and each time I gave the same reply. ⁵The fifth time, Sanballat's servant came with an open letter in his hand, ⁶and this is what it said: "There is a rumor among the surrounding nations, and Geshem tells me it is true, that you and the Jews are planning to rebel and that is why you are building the wall. According to his reports, you plan to be their king. ⁷He also reports that you have appointed prophets in Jerusalem to

proclaim about you, 'Look! There is a king in Judah!' "You can be very sure that this report will get back to the king, so I suggest that you come and talk it over with me." [8] I replied, "There is no truth in any part of your story. You are making up the whole thing." [9] They were just trying to intimidate us, imagining that they could discourage us and stop the work. So I continued the work with even greater determination.

It not only happened to Nehemiah, but this was done to all the Mighty Men of God throughout the bible. It happened to King David with King Saul, it happened to Jesus with Satan, it happened to Joseph with his brothers/Potiphar's wife, it happened to Samson with Delilah, etc. This list can go on and on.

Now stop and ask yourself – do you consider yourself a superhero in this world as a Christian?

Do we have an enemy to constantly fight throughout each day?

Stop and think what's unique about your favorite superhero.

Is it his/her powers? Of course! That is what makes him/her our favorite superhero. The way the superhero wins the battle against the enemy (the bad guy) – is the key in making our Superhero our favorite choice.

We also see the uniqueness about our Mighty Men of God in the bible. The perseverance and the faithfulness to God. Jesus, King David and Abraham are all great examples of this.

Brothers and Sisters, these workshops will also lead you to study out God's Word. When I studied the bible, it helped me define my sin. This allowed me to see who I truly was without God. After studying His Word and building a relationship with Him allowed me to see what a true wretch I really was. I was truly what Paul stated in the book of Romans 7:14-25.

Romans 7:14-25 (NIV)

[14] We know that the law is spiritual; but I am unspiritual, sold as a slave to sin. [15] I do not understand what I do. For what I want to do I do not do, but what I hate I do. [16] And if I do what I do not want to do, I agree that the law is good. [17] As it is, it is no longer I myself who do it, but it is sin living in me. [18] For I know that good itself does not dwell in me, that is, in my sinful nature. For I have the desire to do what is good, but I cannot carry it out. [19] For I do not do the good I want to do, but the evil I do not want to do—this I keep on doing. [20] Now if I do what I do not want to do, it is no longer I who do it, but it is sin living in me that does it. [21] So I find this law at work: Although I want to do good, evil is right there with me. [22] For in my inner being I delight in God's law; [23] but I see another law at work in me, waging war against the law of my mind and making me a

prisoner of the law of sin at work within me. **²⁴ *What a wretched man I am! Who will rescue me from this body that is subject to death? ²⁵ Thanks be to God, who delivers me through Jesus Christ our Lord!*** So then, I myself in my mind am a slave to God's law, but in my sinful nature a slave to the law of sin.

After listing my sin, I seen myself as the greatest villain of all time matched up against God's Word. When I ran across this scripture **1 John 4:4**, I noticed that with God's power I did not have to be the villain anymore in this life.

1 John 4:4 (NLT)

⁴ But you belong to God, my dear children. You have already won a victory over those people, because the Spirit who lives in you is greater than the spirit who lives in the world.

I discovered that building a relationship with Him I could turn my life around and be a superhero in the world and remove my worldly costume. As I started walking with God, joining in on His Gospel League, Satan was no longer my master. God removed the bondage, the chains that Satan had on me.

Brothers and Sisters, please remember that only a higher power (God) can remove those chains.

I had to let God take over my life to help transform me. Please see Romans 12:2 below.

Romans 12:2 (NLT)

Don't copy the behavior and customs of this world, but let God transform you into a new person by changing the way you think. Then you will learn to know God's will for you, which is good and pleasing and perfect.

I was in the world very deep and it felt good. I did not want to come out. I was a "material girl". I had all the fancy cars, clothes, purses, and make-up. I also loved the "bad" boys. The verse, Ephesians 2:2, states that Satan is the ruler of the kingdom of the air, (the ruler of the world).

Ephesians 2:1-9 (NIV)

Made Alive in Christ

[1] As for you, you were dead in your transgressions and sins, [2] ***in which you used to live when you followed the ways of this world and of the ruler of the kingdom of the air, the spirit who is now at work in those who are disobedient.*** [3] All of us also lived among them at one time, gratifying the cravings of our flesh and following its desires and thoughts. Like the rest, we were by nature deserving of wrath. [4] But

because of his great love for us, God, who is rich in mercy, **5** made us alive with Christ even when we were dead in transgressions—it is by grace you have been saved. **6** And God raised us up with Christ and seated us with him in the heavenly realms in Christ Jesus, **7** in order that in the coming ages he might show the incomparable riches of his grace, expressed in his kindness to us in Christ Jesus. **8** For it is by grace you have been saved, through faith—and this is not from yourselves, it is the gift of God— **9** not by works, so that no one can boast.

We need to choose God as our master and not Satan. When we follow Satan, we are being led by evil. See John 8:44 below.

John 8:44 (NLT)

For you are the children of your father the devil, and you love to do the evil things he does. He was a murderer from the beginning. He has always hated the truth, because there is no truth in him. When he lies, it is consistent with his character; for he is a liar and the father of lies.

If you continue to serve Him, you will never discover the Kingdom of God. ***It is a beautiful thing.*** It is a true treasure as stated in Matthew 13:44.

Matthew 13:44 (NLT)

Parables of the Hidden Treasure and the Pearl

"The Kingdom of Heaven is like a treasure that a man discovered hidden in a field. In his excitement, he hid it again and sold everything he owned to get enough money to buy the field.

God was the superhero that rescued and saved me. When I joined His Gospel League, I found myself, learned to love Him, my neighbor, myself, and understand my purpose for being on the planet Earth. Before building on my relationship with Him I was lost and had no clue of my purpose in life. I claimed to be a Christian but after studying the bible and learning of my sin, it helped me to see who I was in this world.

These 6 workshops that I have constructed is the mission that God has assigned to me to help others join His Gospel League and stand for something great in this world, by spreading His Gospel to save the lost. It is to help others witness His Holy Spirit at work within us. Our assignment is to spread His Gospel and to make it to heaven, (eternal life). He states in Philippians 3:20, that we are Citizens of Heaven.

Philippians 3:20 (NLT)

But we are citizens of heaven, where the Lord Jesus Christ lives. And we are eagerly waiting for him to return as our Savior.

1 Peter 2:11 states that we are temporary residents and foreigners of this world. This world is our temporary home.

1 Peter 2:11 (NLT)

Dear friends, I warn you as "temporary residents and foreigners" to keep away from worldly desires that wage war against your very souls.

We have a place waiting for us in heaven. We should not store our treasures here on Earth, again it is not our home. Here are scriptures on what we should treasure:

- ### Matthew 19:21 (NLT)

  Jesus told him, "If you want to be perfect, go and sell all your possessions and give the money to the poor, and you will have treasure in heaven. Then come, follow me."

- ### Mark 10:21 (NLT)

  Looking at the man, Jesus felt genuine love for him. "There is still one thing you haven't done," he told him. "Go and sell all your possessions and give the money to the poor, and you will have treasure in heaven. Then come, follow me."

- **Luke 12:33 (NLT)**

  "Sell your possessions and give to those in need. This will store up treasure for you in heaven! And the purses of heaven never get old or develop holes. Your treasure will be safe; no thief can steal it and no moth can destroy it.

- **Luke 12:34 (NLT)**

  Wherever your treasure is, there the desires of your heart will also be.

- **Luke 18:22 (NLT)**

  When Jesus heard his answer, he said, "There is still one thing you haven't done. Sell all your possessions and give the money to the poor, and you will have treasure in heaven. Then come, follow me."

We have a mission on Earth and that is to help save the lost.

I grew up in a dark world. I was never taught the true meaning of love. I still struggle with being loving today if I take my eyes off God. Before getting to know God, I believe we all suffer from a spiritual illness. We were all born into sin, so it is spiritual blindness. I was truly living in the 'Dark', blinded by sin. Growing up in a violent environment and dysfunctional home is what made me accept this condition. I suffered with this blindness for 34 years before receiving my eyesight, (Jesus Christ) – the Truth.

I had to hold this scripture close at heart, **_John 12:46_**.

> **John 12:46 (NLT),** [46] I have come as a light to shine in this dark world, so that all who put their trust in me will no longer remain in the dark.

I was truly blinded by life. God was my **_"white cane"_** and is to this day. He helped me see through the darkness in which I was born. Before turning to God I was touching things and experiencing things because I had no eyesight. I made choices based off what I was taught. I did not have God's spirit living within me. I did not have his wisdom and knowledge to make the right choices (the smart choices). I had to find my own way in life. I received a spiritual healing that I am so grateful of to this day. And this is the reason that I have decided to stay at Jesus feet, just as Mary Magdalene as mentioned in the bible (in Luke 8:2).

Luke 8:2 (NLT)

[2] along with some women who had been cured of evil spirits and diseases. Among them were

Mary Magdalene, from whom he had cast out seven demons;

He removed seven demonic spirits from Mary Magdalene as stated in the bible. Mary Magdalene had a change of heart when God removed those seven demonic spirits within her. She stayed at Jesus feet, because she never forgot where he took her from. He broke the chains that kept her in bondage with Satan. She never forgot what it was like to have powerful evil spirits living within her that was constantly controlling her.

We were all born into a sinful nature, See the Romans 5:12-21 below.

Romans 5:12-21 (NLT)

Adam and Christ Contrasted

[12] When Adam sinned, sin entered the world. Adam's sin brought death, so death spread to everyone, for everyone sinned. [13] Yes, people sinned even before the law was given. But it was not counted as sin because there was not yet any law to break. [14] Still, everyone died—from the time of Adam to the time of Moses—even those who did not disobey an explicit commandment of God, as Adam did. Now Adam is a symbol, a representation of Christ, who was yet to come. [15] But there is

a great difference between Adam's sin and God's gracious gift. For the sin of this one man, Adam, brought death to many. But even greater is God's wonderful grace and his gift of forgiveness to many through this other man, Jesus Christ. [16] And the result of God's gracious gift is very different from the result of that one man's sin. For Adam's sin led to condemnation, but God's free gift leads to our being made right with God, even though we are guilty of many sins. [17] For the sin of this one man, Adam, caused death to rule over many. But even greater is God's wonderful grace and his gift of righteousness, for all who receive it will live in triumph over sin and death through this one man, Jesus Christ. [18] Yes, Adam's one sin brings condemnation for everyone, but Christ's one act of righteousness brings a right relationship with God and new life for everyone. [19] Because one person disobeyed God, many became sinners. But because one other person obeyed God, many will be made righteous. [20] God's law was given so that all people could see how sinful they were. But as people sinned more and more, God's wonderful grace became more abundant. [21] So just as sin ruled over all people and brought them to death, now God's wonderful grace rules instead, giving us right standing with God and resulting in eternal life through Jesus Christ our Lord.

My life also relates to this story in the bible about the blind beggar. In Luke 18:35-43

It talks about Jesus Healing a Blind Beggar

Luke 18:35-43 (NLT)

[35] As Jesus approached Jericho, a blind beggar was sitting beside the road. [36] When he heard the noise of a crowd going past, he asked what was happening. [37] They told him that Jesus the Nazarene was going by. [38] So he began shouting, "Jesus, Son of David, have mercy on me!" [39] "Be quiet!" the people in front yelled at him. But he only shouted louder, "Son of David, have mercy on me!" [40] When Jesus heard him, he stopped and ordered that the man be brought to him. As the man came near, Jesus asked him, [41] "What do you want me to do for you?"Lord," he said, "I want to see!" [42] And Jesus said, "All right, receive your sight! Your faith has healed you." [43] Instantly the man could see, and he followed Jesus, praising God. And all who saw it praised God, too.

I often wonder why my life was so hard growing up, but I can truly say through all of the hard times God has truly refined my heart into gold.

I now consider myself a superhero in this world as a Christian, as someone who have escaped the dark world (SIN), and on a mission to help others escape.

As a superhero, on God's Gospel League, I learned to wear the full armor of God. This costume, (The Whole Armor of God) has power, because God's Spirit lives within us. It is the only way to fight our enemy, Satan. It comes off, when we take our eyes off God.

Ephesians 6:10-20 (NLT)

The Whole Armor of God

[10] A final word: Be strong in the Lord and in his mighty power. [11] Put on all of God's armor so that you will be able to stand firm against all strategies of the devil. [12] For we are not fighting against flesh-and-blood enemies, but against evil rulers and authorities of the unseen world, against mighty powers in this dark world, and against evil spirits in the heavenly places. [13] Therefore, put on every piece of God's armor so you will be able to resist the enemy in the time of evil. Then after the battle you will still be standing firm. [14] Stand your ground, putting on the belt of truth and the body armor of God's righteousness. [15] For shoes, put on the peace that comes from the Good News so that you will be fully prepared. [16] In addition to

all of these, hold up the shield of faith to stop the fiery arrows of the devil. [17] Put on salvation as your helmet, and take the sword of the Spirit, which is the word of God. [18] Pray in the Spirit at all times and on every occasion. Stay alert and be persistent in your prayers for all believers everywhere. [19] And pray for me, too. Ask God to give me the right words so I can boldly explain God's mysterious plan that the Good News is for Jews and Gentiles alike. [20] I am in chains now, still preaching this message as God's ambassador. So pray that I will keep on speaking boldly for him, as I should.

WORKSHOP 1

ASSIGNMENT: Review Some Marvel Superheroes.

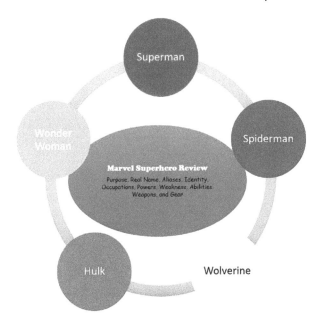

Workshop 1: This is the workshop where you get to review some of the main characteristics about some of the common Marvel Superheroes (Refer to Appendix I). When you go through this review process think about yourself (what are some characteristics that you have when it comes to saving the lost and winning the battles with the Devil).

Homework: Find a comic book scene of your favorite marvel superhero and hold onto it for Workshop 4.

WORKSHOP 2

ASSIGNMENT: Review Some Superheroes from the Bible.

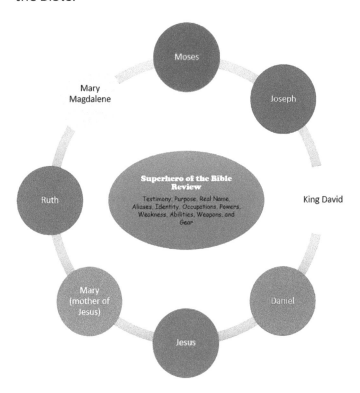

Workshop 2: This workshop will allow you to review the characteristics and abilities of some of the Mighty Women/Men of God from the Bible (Refer to Appendix II). This review will help you understand how powerful we truly are with the Holy Spirit living within

us as Christians. It will help you define your powers, strength, and wonders that we have on God's mission to save the world (winning the souls of the lost) and to fight against the enemy. We were given all this when we decided to make Jesus, Lord of our life (by believing in him and being baptized, in his name). The Holy Spirit is our Counselor that will never leave us.

Read the scriptures below regarding our Counselor, (the Holy Spirit). Can you imagine going through life without a counselor that lives within you – that guides you – and having God's gift of wisdom to help you make the right decisions in life? When you live a life without God, you don't have the Holy Spirit. When you think about it, that really must be a hard life. Jesus had to die first before we could be given His Power (which is the Holy Spirit) living within us. Please read about this in the scriptures listed below.

- ♦ John 14:16 (HCSB) [16] And I will ask the Father, and He will give you another Counselor to be with you forever.

- ♦ John 14:26 (HCSB) [26] But the Counselor, the Holy Spirit—the Father will send Him in My name—will teach you all things and remind you of everything I have told you.

- ♦ John 15:26 (HCSB) [26] "When the Counselor comes, the One I will send to you from the

Father—the Spirit of truth who proceeds from the Father—He will testify about Me.

♦   John 16:7 (NIV) [7] But very truly I tell you, it is for your good that I am going away. Unless I go away, the Advocate will not come to you; but if I go, I will send him to you..

♦   Romans 11:34 (NIV) "Who has known the mind of the Lord? Or who has been his counselor?"

♦   Acts 2:16-21 (NLT) [16] No, what you see was predicted long ago by the prophet Joel:

[17] 'In the last days,' God says, 'I will pour out my Spirit upon all people. Your sons and daughters will prophesy. Your young men will see visions, and your old men will dream dreams.

[18] In those days I will pour out my Spirit even on my servants—men and women alike—and they will prophesy. [19] And I will cause wonders in the heavens above and signs on the earth below—blood and fire and clouds of smoke.

[20] The sun will become dark, and the moon will turn blood red before that great and glorious day of the Lord arrives. [21] But everyone who calls on the name of the Lord will be saved.'

♦ Acts 2:32-35 (NLT)

[32] "God raised Jesus from the dead, and we are all witnesses of this. [33] Now he is exalted to the place of highest honor in heaven, at God's right hand. And the Father, as he had promised, gave him the Holy Spirit to pour out upon us, just as you see and hear today. [34] For David himself never ascended into heaven, yet he said, 'The Lord said to my Lord,

"Sit in the place of honor at my right hand [35] until I humble your enemies, making them a footstool under your feet.'"

Jesus is the Most High Superhero – who also gave us His power to become superheroes.

Homework: Review your life as a Christian and make the same list of characteristics and abilities that you reviewed of the Superheroes of the Bible.

WORKSHOP 3

ASSIGNMENT: Pair up with someone in the workshop and share your characteristics and abilities as a Christian that you completed for the Workshop 2 homework. This list should consist of the following: Testimony, Purpose, Real Name, Spiritual Gifts/ Abilities, Occupations, Strengths, Weakness, and Spiritual Weapons.

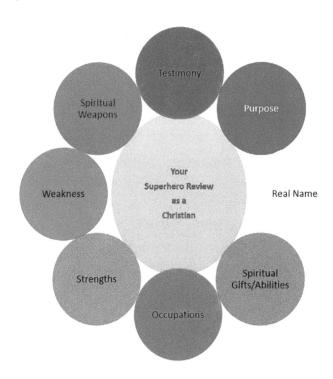

Workshop 3: This workshop will allow you to dig into your past – go back to your testimony (See the Template in: Appendix II)– which gives you a format to follow to help you define: who you were before you gained your superhero powers (the Holy Spirit) and who you truly are without God's power (the Holy Spirit). This review will also help you define who the enemy is (Satan) and his army, that comes and intimidates you while you are on God's mission. What are some of the things that make you weak in your soul—while living out God's Mission—to save the lost?

Take out the time to answer the questions below and brainstorm about your characteristics and abilities as a Christian. The below list of questions will give you a starting point to begin.

1. Who do you go to, to get your strength?
2. Who is the enemy (your enemy)?
3. What gives you daily strength?
4. Who are the other teammates on your team?
5. What shield of protection are you putting on each day (What suit are you wearing)?
6. Is your suit always on or do you hide yourself – by taking your suit off?? Do you hide your light away? Do you allow others to see your light?
7. Brainstorm about yourself (after your Spiritual Birth in Christ - as a Christian)

8. Write out your testimony.
9. Who were you before?
10. How were you found?
11. Where were you when that someone reached out to you?

WORKSHOP 4

ASSIGNMENT: Share your favorite marvel comic strip or favorite story of a mighty man/woman of God from the bible.

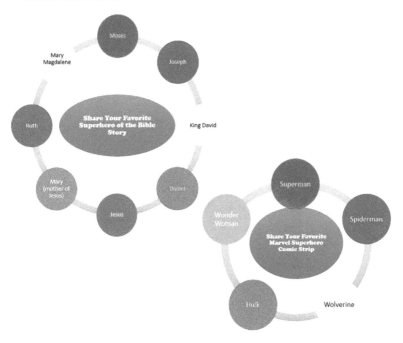

Workshop 4: In this workshop you will share a story or a comic strip from your greatest Biblical Superhero or Marvel Superhero.

Homework: Create your own comic strip based on a life that you have saved (helped someone become a Christian) or someone who you have showed compassion for. Please also make up a superhero character for yourself from the Marvel Superhero Review, which includes: (a Purpose, Real Name, Aliases, Identity, Occupations, Powers, Weakness, Abilities, Weapons, and Gear) or you can list your characteristics and abilities as a Christian, which includes your: (Testimony, Purpose, Real Name, Spiritual Gifts/ Abilities, Occupations, Strengths, Weakness, and Spiritual Weapons)

WORKSHOP 5

ASSIGNMENT: Share your own comic strip based on a life that you have saved (helped someone become a Christian) or someone who you have showed compassion for. Please also share the superhero character that you have created for yourself from the Marvel Superhero Review, which includes: (a Purpose, Real Name, Aliases, Identity, Occupations, Powers, Weakness, Abilities, Weapons, and Gear) or you can list your characteristics and abilities as a Christian, which includes your: (Testimony, Purpose, Real Name, Spiritual Gifts/Abilities, Occupations, Strengths, Weakness, and Spiritual Weapons)

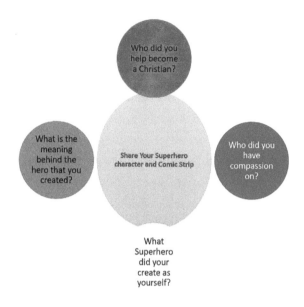

Who did you help become a Christian?

What is the meaning behind the hero that you created?

Share Your Superhero character and Comic Strip

Who did you have compassion on?

What Superhero did your create as yourself?

Here is a link to create a superhero:

https://www.youtube.com/watch?v=7yL8DGB7YC0
https://www.wikihow.com/Create-a-Super-Hero

Workshop 5: In this workshop, you will present a comic strip and a superhero character that you have created for yourself that defines your characteristics and abilities as a Superhero in this world as a Christian.

Homework: Celebrate with a party for Workshop 6. Please have a T-Shirt made of the Superhero Character that you created for yourself on the front. On the back place your Biblical and Marvel superhero (split the two). Please wear this T-Shirt to the party.

WORKSHOP 6

ATTEND THE PARTY Celebration for Workshop 6. Please have a T-Shirt made of the Superhero Character that you created for yourself on the front. On the back place your Biblical and Marvel superhero (split the two). Please wear this T-Shirt to the party.

Workshop 6: This workshop will allow you to celebrate your accomplishment. You are required to wear a T-Shirt that you have designed with your favorite Marvel Superhero and your favorite Biblical Superhero (side-by-side) on the back of the T-Shirt and the superhero that you created of the image of yourself as a Christian on the front of the T-Shirt.

Appendix I –
Main Characteristics of common Marvel Superheroes

About Superman

SUPERMAN is a native of Krypton, a planet that had a red sun, under a yellow sun.

Superman is a fictional character, a comic book superhero who appears in comic books published by DC Comics. He is widely considered to be an American cultural icon. Created by American writer Jerry Siegel and Canadian-born American artist Joe Shuster in 1932 while both were living in Cleveland, Ohio, and sold to Detective Comics, Inc. (later DC Comics) in 1938, the character first appeared in *Action Comics* #1 (June 1938) and subsequently appeared in various radio serials, television programs, films, newspaper strips, and video games. With the success of his adventures, Superman helped to create the superhero genre and establish its primacy within the American comic book. The character's appearance is distinctive and iconic: a blue, red and yellow costume, complete with cape, with a stylized "S" shield on his chest. This shield is now typically used across media to symbolize the character.

The origin story of Superman relates that he was born **Kal-El** on the planet Krypton, before being rocketed to Earth as an infant by his scientist father Jor-El, moments before Krypton's destruction. Discovered and adopted by a Kansas farmer and his wife, the child is raised as **Clark Kent** and imbued with a strong moral compass. Very early he started to display superhuman abilities, which upon reaching maturity he resolved to use for the benefit of humanity.

Superman has fascinated scholars, with cultural theorists, commentators, and critics alike exploring the character's impact and role in the United States and the rest of the world. Umberto Eco discussed the mythic qualities of the character in the early 1960s, and Larry Niven has pondered the implications of a sexual relationship involving the character. The character's ownership has often been the subject of dispute, with Siegel and Shuster twice suing for the return of legal ownership. Superman placed first on IGN's Top 100 Comic Book Heroes in May 2011.

His Powers

- Like that of Earth's his Kryptonian cells act as living solar batteries, absorbing solar energy and giving him superhuman powers.

- He possesses tremendous strength; while Superman's strength is not infinite, its full extent is so great that it has never been accurately measured.

- His body is virtually indestructible.

- Superman's sharp senses enable him to hear sounds too faint to be detected by the normal human ear.

- His "telescopic vision" enables him to focus his sight on distant objects far beyond the range of normal human sight.

- His "microscopic vision" allows him to observe an object in microscopic detail.

- Superman's so called "x-ray vision" enables him to see clearly through solid objects. Certain dense materials notably lead, obstruct this ability.

- His power to generate heat within objects manifests itself as a red glow within his eyes, and is therefore known as "heat vision."

- Superman can move, react, and think at superhuman speeds greater than that of sound.

- He can defy gravity and fly through force of will.

- Superman's irradiated cells generate a force field that extends for a fraction of an inch around his body, rendering any material within the field nearly indestructible, such as his skin tight costume. (Because his cape extends beyond the field, it is easily damaged.)

His Weakness

- Superman is vulnerable to the radiation of Kryptonite, a substance from his native planet.

- Kryptonite radiation will kill Superman within minutes.

- He is also vulnerable to magic, and to the sonic powers of some beings, such as Braniac.

- Superman must fill his lungs with air before flying through outer space.

- He can thus survive without breathing for several hours, but ultimately, he must replenish his oxygen supply to remain alive.

About Spiderman

REAL NAME: Peter Benjamin Parker. His identity is "secret". His occupation is Freelance photographer; former assistant high school coach, science teacher, scientific researcher. Peter Peter is an accomplished scientist, inventor and photographer.

Spider-Man is a fictional character, a comic book superhero who appears in comic books published by Marvel Comics. Created by writer-editor Stan Lee and writer-artist Steve Ditko, he first appeared in *Amazing Fantasy* #15 (August 1962). Lee and Ditko conceived the character as an orphan being raised by his Aunt May and Uncle Ben, and as a teenager, having to deal with the normal struggles of adolescence in addition to those of a costumed crimefighter. Spider-Man's creators gave him super strength and agility, the ability to cling to most surfaces, shoot spider-webs using devices of his own invention which he called "web-shooters", and react to danger quickly with his "spider-sense", enabling him to combat his foes.

When Spider-Man first appeared in the early 1960s, teenagers in superhero comic books were usually relegated to the role of sidekick to the protagonist. The Spider-Man series broke ground by featuring **Peter Parker**, a teenage high school student and person behind Spider-Man's secret identity to whose "self-obsessions with rejection, inadequacy, and loneliness" young readers could relate. Unlike previous teen heroes such as Bucky and Robin, Spider-Man did not benefit from being the protégé of any adult superhero mentors like Captain America and Batman, and thus had to learn for himself that "with great power there must also come great responsibility"—a line included in a text box in the final panel of the first Spider-Man story, but later retroactively attributed to his guardian, the late Uncle Ben.

Aliases: Friendly Neighborhood Spider-Man, the Amazing Spider-Man, the Sensational Spider-Man, the Spectacular Spider-Man, "Tiger," Spidey, Webhead, Webslinger, Wall-crawler, "Little Man"; formerly "the Amazing Octo-Spidey", Bag-Man, "Bookworm," Captain Universe, Dusk, Hornet, Mad Dog #336, Man-Spider, Prodigy, "Puny Parker," Ricochet, Scarlet Spider, Spider-Hulk, Spider-Phoenix.

His Powers

- Peter can cling to most surfaces, has superhuman strength (able to lift 10 tons optimally) and is roughly 15 times more agile than a regular human. The combination of his acrobatic leaps and web-slinging enables him to travel rapidly from place to place.

- His spider-sense provides an early warning detection system linked with his superhuman kinesthetics, enabling him the ability to evade most any injury, provided he doesn't cognitively override the autonomic reflexes.

- Note: his power enhancements through his transformation by the Queen and after battling Morlun - including his organic web glands and stingers - have been undone after Spider-Man's deal with Mephisto.

His costume

- Spider-Man designed and constructed several devices that he traditionally carries as part of his full costume. This includes twin artificial web-shooters worn at the wrists, spare web cartridges attached to his belt, spider-tracer devices attuned to his spider-sense, the spider-signal light, and a compact camera.

- He has reconstructed his web shooters out of a high density plastic to avoid metal detectors, and has added modifications to detect low web-fluid levels, and propel spider-tracers.

- For a time while allied with Iron Man, Spider-Man wore a costume that was equipped with filters in the mouth area to keep out toxins and allow him to breathe underwater, audio amplification, visual amplification (including vision in the infrared and ultraviolet wavelengths), a short-range GPS microwave communication system (with a built-in fire, police, and emergency scanner), and retractable webbing under his arms that allow short bursts of gliding.

- The costume was made of a material that could serve as a bulletproof jacket against small caliber bullets. For the first upgrade to the costume, Stark added three mechanical waldo arms, which can grab and move objects as well housing cameras which transmit images back to the costume's eyepiece.

- The waldoes can also be used offensively in combat. The costume is now built out of a liquid metal nanofiber material allowing it to quickly change in appearance upon mental command into anything from Spider-Man's civilian clothes to his former costumes, as well as providing camouflage by blending with the surrounding colors.

About Hulk:

REAL NAME: Robert Bruce Banner - Unemployed, former nuclear physicist Dr. Bruce Banner is a genius in nuclear physics, possessing a mind so brilliant that it cannot be measured on any known intelligence test. When Banner is the Hulk, Banner's consciousness is buried within the Hulk's, and can influence the Hulk's behavior only to a very limited extent.

The **Hulk** is a fictional character, a superhero who appears in comic books published by Marvel Comics. Created by Stan Lee and Jack Kirby, the character first appeared in *The Incredible Hulk* #1 (cover-dated May 1962). He is a gigantic, green, irradiated, mutated humanoid monster with incredible strength and an inability to control his rage. The Hulk is sometimes characterized as hyper-aggressive and brutal, while at other times as cunning, brilliant, and scheming. He is often portrayed as an antihero. The Hulk is cast as the emotional and impulsive alter ego of the withdrawn and reserved physicist **Dr. Robert Bruce Banner**. Banner first transforms into the Hulk shortly after he is accidentally exposed to the blast of a test detonation of a gamma bomb he invented. Subsequently, Banner will involuntarily transform into the Hulk whenever he gets too angry or if his life is in danger, leading to extreme complications in Banner's life. Lee said the Hulk's creation was inspired by a combination of *Dr. Jekyll and Mr. Hyde* and *Frankenstein*.

Although the Hulk's coloration has varied throughout the character's publication history, the most consistent shade is green. As the Hulk, Banner is capable of significant feats of strength, the magnitude of which increase in direct proportion to the character's anger. As the character himself puts it, "The madder Hulk gets, the stronger Hulk gets!" Strong emotions such as anger, terror and grief are also triggers for forcing Banner's transformation into the Hulk. As a child, Banner's father Brian Banner often got mad and physically abused his mother, creating the psychological complex of fear, anger, and the fear of anger and the destruction it can cause that underlies the character. A common storyline is the pursuit of both Banner and the Hulk by the U.S. armed forces, because of all the destruction that he causes. He has two main catchphrases: "Hulk is strongest there is!" and the better-known "HULK SMASH!", which has founded the basis for a number of pop culture memes.

Aliases: Annihilator, Captain Universe, Joe Fixit, Mr. Fixit, Mechano, Professor, War, Bruce Bancroft, David Banner, David Bixby, Bob Danner, Bruce Jones, Bruce Roberts, David Blaine, the Green Scar, Green Goliath, Jade Giant, Bob

His Powers:

- The Hulk possesses an incredible level of superhuman physical ability. His capacity for physical strength is potentially limitless due to the fact that the Hulk's strength increases proportionally with his level of great emotional stress, anger in particular.

- The Hulk uses his superhumanly strong leg muscles to leap great distances. The Hulk has been known to cover hundreds of miles in a single bound and once leaped almost into orbit around the Earth.

- The Hulk has shown a high resistance to physical damage nearly regardless of the cause, and has also shown resistance to extreme temperatures, poisons, and diseases in addition to regeneration of damaged or destroyed areas of tissue at an amazing rate.

- The Hulk's body also has a gland that makes an "oxygenated per fluorocarbon emulsion", which creates pressure in the Hulk's lungs and effectively lets him breathe underwater and move quickly between varying depths without concerns about decompression or nitrogen narcosis.

About Wolverine

REAL NAME: James Howlett, Adventurer, instructor, former bartender, bouncer, spy, government operative, mercenary, soldier, sailor, miner, Secret, known to certain government agencies,

Due to his extensive training as a soldier, a C.I.A. operative, a samurai, a spy, and a member of the X-Men, Wolverine is an exceptional hand-to-hand combatant, having mastered virtually every fighting style on Earth. He is also a trained expert in multiple types of weapons, vehicles, computer systems, explosives, and assassination techniques.

Wolverine is fluent in many languages, including Japanese, Russian, Chinese, Cheyenne, Lakota, and Spanish; he has some knowledge of French, Thai, and Vietnamese.

Wolverine is a fictional character, a superhero who appears in comic books published by Marvel Comics. Born

James Howlett and commonly known as **Logan**, Wolverine is a mutant who possesses animal-keen senses, enhanced physical capabilities, three retracting bone claws on each hand and a healing factor that allows him to recover from virtually any wound, disease, or toxin at an accelerated rate. The healing factor also slows down his aging process, enabling him to live beyond a normal human lifespan. His powerful healing factor enabled the supersoldier program Weapon X to bond the near-indestructible metal alloy adamantium to his skeleton and claws without killing him. He is most often depicted as a member of the X-Men, Alpha Flight, or later the Avengers.

Aliases: Logan, formerly Weapon Ten, Death, Mutate #9601, Jim Logan, Patch, Canucklehead, Emilio Garra, Weapon Chi, Weapon X, Experiment X, Agent Ten, Canada, Wildboy, Peter Richards, many others

His Powers:

- Wolverine is a mutant who possesses the ability to regenerate damaged or destroyed areas of his cellular structure at a rate far greater than that of an ordinary human.

- The speed at which this healing factor works varies in direct proportion with the severity of the damage Wolverine suffers. For example, he can fully recover from an ordinary gunshot wound in a non-vital area of his body within minutes, but it took him almost two months to fully recover from injuries sustained in a duel with Lord Shingen, which included one from a sword that went all the way through his trunk.

- Wolverine's natural healing also affords him virtual immunity to poisons and most drugs, as well as an enhanced resistance to diseases. For example, it is nearly impossible for him to become intoxicated from drinking alcohol. He also has a limited immunity to the fatigue poisons generated by bodily activity, and hence he has greater endurance than an ordinary human. His agility and reflexes are similarly enhanced.

- In addition, Wolverine's healing factor provides him with an extended lifespan by slowing the effects of the aging process. Although over a century old, Wolverine is as healthy and physically fit as a man in his prime.

- Wolverine also possesses superhumanly acute senses, making him capable of seeing things at a maximum distance greater than a normal human's. His hearing is enhanced in a similar manner, and he is able to recognize people and objects by scent, even if that person or object is hidden.

- Wolverine can use these enhanced senses to track any creature with an impressive degree of success.

- Wolverine's skeleton includes six retractable one-foot long bone claws, three in each arm, that are housed beneath the skin and muscle of his forearms. Wolverine can, at will, release these slightly curved claws through his skin beneath the knuckles on each hand. The skin between the knuckles tears and bleeds, but the blood loss is quickly halted by his healing factor.

- Wolverine can unsheathe any number of his claws at once, although he must keep his wrists straight at the moment his claws shoot from his forearms into his hands. When unsheathed, the claws are fully within his hands, and thus Wolverine can still bend his wrists.

- The claws are naturally sharp and tougher than that of normal human bone structure, allowing Wolverine to cut through most types of flesh and natural materials.

- Despite the extent of his healing factor, Wolverine is not immortal. If the injuries are extensive enough, especially if they result in the loss of vital organs, large amounts of blood, and/or loss of physical form, such as having flesh burned away by fire or acid, Wolverine can die

His Costume:

- Wolverine's entire skeletal structure, including his claws, has been artificially bonded to the nearly indestructible metal Adamantium. As a result, Wolverine's bones are virtually unbreakable, and his claws are capable of cutting through almost any substance depending on its thickness and the amount of force he can exert.

- Due to his healing factor, the presence of Adamantium in his body does not interfere with his bones' normal function of generating blood corpuscles. The reinforcement of his skeleton enables Wolverine to withstand high levels of physical pressure, giving his muscles sufficient force to briefly lift/press several hundred pounds.

- Throughout his life, Wolverine has used a variety of bladed weapons, most frequently daggers and, at times, swords. He has also wielded many different types of firearms throughout his careers as a soldier, a mercenary, and a spy.

About WonderWoman:

REAL NAME: Diana of Themyscira

She is an Amazon, raised on Paradise Island (or Themyscira) who journeys to man's world on a mission of peace. There have been various other aspects of this origin which have stayed mostly as canon, though no longer do. She was originally created of clay after her mother prayed to the god's for a child and her reason for going to man's world was because of the unexpected visit of Steve Trevor to Paradise Island. In the golden age this led to an infatuation with the character that remained for her entire golden and silver age appearances. After Crisis on Infinite Earths, the character's origin was slightly retold by George Perez. In this version the Amazons were in fact reborn from the souls of abused and murdered women from ancient days. Hippolyta, the leader of the Amazons and Diana's mother, was the sole member of the Amazons who had been pregnant and when it was deemed appropriate the soul of the child was released into the world. Upon this occurring the female goddesses as well as Hermes who had protected her soul in the Cavern of Souls also blessed the soul with powers beyond those of the other Amazons.

Aliases: Diana Prince, Diana of Themyscira, Princess Diana, Princess of the Amazons, Goddess of Truth, Diana the Goddess of Truth, Wondy, Wonder Girl

Occupation

Adventurer, Emissary to the world of Man, Protector of Paradise Island; former Goddess of Truth; former government special agent

Creation

Wonder Woman's appearance in the early golden age of comics made her the first prominent female superheroine. The psychologist William Moulton Marston created Wonder Woman somewhat as a counter reaction to the presence of prominent male superheroes (at this time Superman, Batman and Captain America) with the hopes that the character could serve as an inspiration for young children (though in certain ways it was geared more towards female readers.) Marston had been partially motivated to creating this character because of the accomplishments of his own wife, who was also an accomplished academic in a time when it was difficult for women to fulfill this role.

Character Evolution

As one of the longest running comic book characters, Diana has seen a great deal of development and throughout every era of comics.

The New 52
Wonder Woman

The character's depiction in the new 52 has been mostly along the same lines as the remainder of her modern appearances, though as of yet much remains to be explained about her character. One development with the character in this new universe is that some of the developments which occurred during Flashpoint are occasionally referenced (such as her using London as her base of operations.)

Continuity Problems

Due to the reboot of the character following Crisis on Infinite Earths, numerous things no longer made sense in terms of continuity as it related to the remainder of the DC Universe. As her first overall appearance was now in continuity around the Legends miniseries, it no longer made sense that she was a founding member of the Justice League of America. This founding position was instead given retroactively to Black Canary. Later it was decided that she should be given this position back and thus both she and Black Canary were considered founding members of the Justice League. In reference to the Justice League though, although she has more than 400 combined appearances therein, she has had most of her character development in her own series.

Relationship with Superman
Justice League 12

Although she has traditionally paired with either Steve Trevor or no one as a main romatnic lead, and Superman with either Lois Land or Lana Lang, there has often been the hint of a romance between the two characters. This began in the 1960 in the series Superman's Girlfriend, Lois Lane which was equal parts romance and action themed. In order to drive along the romance, the theme often came up of Lois Lane believing that Superman really loved Wonder Woman (though this was mostly for the purposes of a case.) In later years the same ideas perpetuated though most in imaginary stories or alternate tellings of the future. Following Crisis on Infinite Earths the characters were briefly linked romantically in Action Comic #600 which was written by John Byrne. Subsequently the characters' interest in one another was generally portrayed as a strong friendship (this occurred under different writers, primarily Messner-Loebs and Rucka.) Following the reboot of the DC universe into the new 52 the characters once again showed a romantic interest in one another. They found common ground in the isolation which their power give them and shared a kiss in Justice League #12 in 2012.

Powers and Abilities

Wonder Woman's powers are as a result of her blessings by the gods (or presumably in the modern version by her divine ancestry.) Her abilities in large part come from her upbringing in the martial society of the Amazons.

Superhuman strength

Her level of superstrength (as granted to her by Demeter) is comparable to that of the Earth itself (as this is where she derives her powers.) She is thus strong on a level with the strongest other DC's characters including Superman and Captain Marvel. It is generally accepted that she is not as strong as Superman, but that she is one of the few in the same class as he is. On one occasion she even used her massive strength to move the Earth (though this was under duress and aided by Superman and the Martian Manhunter.)

Superhuman Speed

As granted by Hermes, this speed has never been well documented, but she has been shown to be on par with some of the fastest characters in the DC Universe. She can disarm human opponents of their weapons in seconds, and is such a well trained athlete that in combat, her reflexes even surprise the likes of Superman.

Invulnerability

Although she is immune to radiation and the coldness of space, piercing weapons and hot temperatures can have an effect on her.

Flight

Also granted by Hermes, this ability allows her to fly at fast speeds. In the silver age she could not fly and had to rely on the Amazon ability to glide on air currents and her invisible plane.

Healing factor

In the rare instance when Wonder Woman is harmed, her body heals from any injury instantly without scarring

Divine Wisdom

Granted by Athena, this gives her a degree of wisdom beyond that of most mortals and gives her a strong moral sense. This also aids her in her tactical ability.

Great beauty

Although not a real power in itself, she received a blessing of great beauty from Aphrodite.

Other assorted divine powers

For a time she was given enhanced vision by Athena, which gave her the ability to see in darkness and through illusions. Due to her wisdom she can learn languages faster than a regular person. She has also been shown to project herself astrally in order to commune with the gods and ask for special favors from them. She has also been shown to take on the abilities of certain of her patron goddesses as when she became a form of divine midwife to save the life of an unborn child.

Martial Combat

Wonder Woman is trained in the a variety of martial arts, making her a master of unarmed and armed combat (even proving adept with pistols.) Even when depowered she is on par with some of the best hand to hand fighters in the DC Universe.

Weapons and Equipment
Lasso of Truth

The Lasso of Truth forces people to tell the truth. It was forged by Hephaestus from the Golden Girdle of Gaea that Antiope had once worn. It is able to restore people's lost memories get rid of illusions or cause illusions to those it holds and heal the holder's body cure insanity and protect people who are in close proximity to it from magical attacks. In the golden age version the lasso could also take on a rigid form and hold people aloft from a great distance away. During these eras, the lasso also forced those who were bound by it to act as the holder demanded. This trait also affected Wonder Woman. A non-combat application of the lasso is that it can be used to change Diana's clothes as long as those clothes are "in the right frequency" as the lasso. Although this was a plot device used more often in the golden and silver age in has been used on occasion in modern comics as for instance one time Diana transformed into a Miss America costume.

Bracelets of Victory

These are a pair of steel cuffs that are indestructible because they were created from the remains of Zeus's Aegis shield. Wonder Woman can use her super reflexes to deflect projectiles, blades, punches, or any form of offensive attack used against her (including Darkseid's Omega Beams.) She can also use them to deflect an object back into her enemies. When Diana crosses them to protect her from impact with larger projectiles as well as damage inflicted by explosions and collisions with hard surfaces, the bracelets generate a small energy shield. In recent events, Diana has learned how to emit a devastating magic lightning attack from her bracelets do to their link with Zeus. This attack can even strike Gods and Goddesses down with a powerful strike, and this attack can even work underwater. In the golden age these were items of submission meant to control Amazons. If they were removed from an Amazon, she would launch into an uncontrollable rage, releasing her full power (this was a plot device which subdued many foes, among them the Crimson Centipede.) Also during this era, if they were bound together by a man, all her powers were lost, this was only true in the Golden Age.

Royal Tiara

Her tiara is razor sharp and can be used so as to return to her when thrown. It is also magical and can therefore be used to injure those susceptible to magic, such as Superman.

The Invisible Plane

The invisible plane was Diana's major means of travel during the Golden and Silver ages as the character did not have the ability of flight. It was controlled telepathically and would appear almost instantly. With the introduction of the power of flight to the character it was a forgotten element of her character until she found the Lansinar Disk. This disc was a piece of alien technology which allowed her to create an invisible version of whatever object or vehicle she visualized it to be. She would use this to create an invisible plane, but it eventually became to be used more to create the Wonder Dome.

Battle Armour

When faced with a larger threat, Diana will wear her Amazon battle armour for added protection as well as use martial weapons such as swords. Technically speaking as well, as reimagined under the George Perez 1980s reboot, the iconic costume is in fact simply the breastplate of this armour. She will also additionally use a shield for added defense when she deems it necessary.

Martial Weapons

Diana is depicted as quite skilled in a number of martial weapons. She has shown to be adept with swords, battle axes and spears. She tends to favour swords though in particularly difficult fights. Her knowledge of martial weapons extends to other less conventional weapons, including broken bottles.

Magical Sword

On occasions Wonder Woman has employed a magical sword of unknown (though presumably Amazon) origin. This sword has been used most specifically against those with the power of invulnerability as invulnerability generally does not work against magical items. It is generally represented as a short sword. In Wonder Woman (vol. 4) #15, Hephaestus modifies Diana's bracelets so that she can manifest two short swords from them during battle.

Sandals of Hermes

Given to Diana by Hermes, these are no longer in canon, but at one point allowed her to travel between Themyscira and the outside world. These sandals have also been given to Artemis and Cassandra Sandsmark as they also provide the power of flight.

Gauntlet of Atlas

These gauntlets allow the strength of any who uses them to be increased by ten. She has used these to battle the White Magician in his demon form and Doomsday. When using them Diana has trouble controlling her sudden increase in strength.

Earrings

Although seemingly only a purely decorative aspect of her costume, in the golden and silver ages, her earrings were sometimes depicted as giving her the ability to breathe in outer space. Gelignite Grenade Earrings and Grappling Hook Bracelet - In her depowered mod girl phase, Diana on rare occasion employed these devices, which were concealed to look like regular parts of her costume. She acquired them from a demolitions expert and villain which she had helped reform. The grenades were strong enough to blast through a thick steel door and the grappling hook could support easily her body weight to aid in climbing.

Power Rings

For a short time during the Blackest Night crossover, Wonder Woman was empowered by a Black Power Ring and then a violet Power Ring.

Depiction and the Iconic Costume

Wonder Woman's costume has come under heavy criticism throughout the years. Many find that as an example of a character that is supposed to represent female empowerment that by wearing a costume which reveals a gratuitous amount of skin that the character is being contradictory. Numerous attempts have been made to make her costume more realistic, however in terms of the character's history there are few problems with it. Despite that it offers little protection, Wonder Woman does not require very much protection, either from harm or from the elements. The costume is also sometimes criticized for its symbolism closely related to American themes, that despite the fact that she is meant to be an emissary of peace to the whole planet, that her costume looks very American This is explained as one of the motivations for her role in man's world. The costume is a breastplate inspired by the colors and symbols of a downed World War II airplane being flown by Steve Trevor's mother . As an American pilot, it is therefore not surprising that stars (on the lower part of her breastplate) and stripes (one her boots) are evident parts of the design. In the summer of 2011, it was announced that DC Comics would reboot its entire lineup and create the new 52. Debate immediately surfaced as the head creative force behind the reboot (Jim Lee) decided that all female characters should be drawn with "pants" or full leg covering as part of their costume. This was in line with the redrawn Wonder Woman after issue #600 in volume 3. However, as the summer progressed images began to appear with Diana in a costume which appeared to be a synthesis of her traditional one and the reimagined one. With the actual reboot this is the costume that was decided on, essentially with the breastplate in the general shape of the traditional costume, and the theme being more in line with the redesign of the previous year. She additionally has added aspects of her uniform which didn't exist before such as a braided armband.

Appendix II –

Characteristics and Abilities of the Mighty Women/Men of God from the Bible

About King David

I SAMUEL 16:1

DAVID WAS THE youngest son of Jesse. From the time David was a little boy, it was his job to look after the sheep. He loved the little lambs. He was a very good shepherd. David was happy keeping the sheep. He liked to be out in the fields, roaming the hills, just him and the clouds, the birds and the trees. Often, he would carry his harp to the fields and sit on the grass. He liked to sing and play music on his harp. The sheep liked it too. Singing and writing songs of praise, little

David looked after the lambs. He was the keeper of his father's sheep. One day, as looked after the sheep, a bear came into the sheep fold. It caught a little lamb. David heard the lamb's cry. He ran after the bear. God made David strong. He took the lamb out of the bears mouth and killed the bear.

Once a lion came into the fold and stole a sheep from out of the flock. David went out and found the lion, with the lamb still in its mouth. He grabbed the lion by the beard and smote him. He killed the lion dead and delivered the lamb safely, from out of its mouth. Singing songs and playing his harp, praising God all the while. David faithfully looked after the sheep. One day word came to the people. A great prophet was coming to town. There was going to be a feast. Jesse called for his sons. It was an important day of worship. The presence of Jesse and his sons was both required and expected. The precious flock was roaming, grazing up on the hill. So, it was imperative one of them should stay behind.

Since, David was the youngest and he so loved the sheep, Jesse appointed him. It was his beloved duty, to care for the flock. Young David would look after the ewes, while they mothered the baby lambs. He would ensure, they came to no harm. When Jesse arrived at the feast, with his seven sons. The old prophet told him, "God has sent me to you. He has chosen one of your sons. I will pour oil, on the head of God's anointed. One day he will be king." All seven sons walked by Samuel. They came one by one. The oldest came first. He was a fine-looking young man. Samuel thought, surely this must be him. But God said, "This is not the one." Twice, each son walked by Samuel. Though, God did not choose any of them.

Finally, God's prophet asked Jesse, "Is this all the sons you have?" Jesse told him, "No, I have one more. But he is just a boy. I left him out in the field. David is my youngest and he watches after my sheep." Samuel said, "Send for him. For we will not sit down, until he comes hither." So, Jesse sent for David. David hurried home to wash and get dressed. Doing his father's bidding, he headed for the feast. David had a beautiful countenance. He was very good to look upon. Samuel watched and waited.

When he saw David coming, he heard the voice of the Lord saying, "This is he. This is the one I have chosen. Anoint him." Samuel, took the horn of oil and poured it on his head. The Holy Spirit came upon David, it dwelt on him, from that day forward. The anointing was done in secret. Years went by, before David actually became king. When David was just a young man Saul was king. Saul became sick and was tormented by an evil spirit. This vexed his servants. They decided, music might sooth him. David played the harp and came highly recommended. Saul's servants had heard many good things about David.

They heard he was cunning in music and that he was both mighty and valiant. This son of Jesse was a prudent man and more than that, the Lord was with him. Then Saul sent messengers to Jesse saying, "Send me thy son, which is with the sheep." So David played his harp for the king. The sound of the harp was soft and soothing. Thus David found favor with Saul, for his music refreshed him. The evil spirit departed from him and he felt well again. David became the chief musician and armor bearer for the King.

During one of the battles David brings food to his brothers. He hears a challenge being made. A challenge for the Israelites to send a champion to decide the outcome of the battle in single combat. David insists that he can defeat Goliath. Young David killed the giant Goliath with a simple stone from his sling. The Philistines flee in terror and the Israelites win a great victory. David brings the head of Goliath and presents it to the king.

Saul makes David a commander over his armies and gives him his daughter Michal in marriage. The people of Israel loved David. The women would dance and sing saying, "Saul has killed his thousands and David has killed his tens of thousands." Saul had a son named Jonathan. Jonathan and David became best friends.

Jonathanloved David as much as he did his own soul. He made a covenant with David. He gave David his robe, his sword and his bow.

Saul became very jealous and vexed at all this. He tried to kill David many times, with his javelin. The evil spirit would come upon King Saul and he would imagine wicked things. Saul and Jonathan died the same day. Jonathan died at the hands of their enemy, the Philistines. A hard battle was fought against Saul and his sons. The men of Israel fled, though many were slain.

Saul was wounded by the archers. He begged his armor bearer to kill him, but he would not. So Saul fell upon his own sword, trying to kill himself. Still, it did not work. He was killed by a stranger. An Amalekite found him near death. Saul asked him, "Slay me I pray." The giant man could see, King Saul's life was fading fast. Thus, he stood upon him and slew him. He brought David the crown of King Saul and the bracelet Saul wore on his arm.

David rent his clothes and asked him, "Were you not afraid to slay God's anointed?" David killed the stranger. He rent his clothes and mourned the death of Jonathan and King Saul. Though, not long after the death of Saul, David was crowned king. David was thirty years old when he began to reign. He was Israel's second and mightiest king.

David was responsible for bringing the "Ark of the Covenant" to Jerusalem. He assembled thirty thousand men to escort the Ark, with music and dancing and much thanksgiving, the Ark was brought forth. David's greatest sin, was in the death of Uriah. He saw Uriah's wife and fell deeply in love. He could not resist Bathsheba. So, he had Uriah sent to the front lines, to fight in the midst of the hottest part of the battle. David knew in his heart it would surely mean, the death of Uriah.

God's punishment for this terrible sin, was in the loss of their first born child. Though, God saw fit to blessed their union with another child. A child named Solomon. Solomon would be Israel's next king. He was the son of David's most beloved wife. David had many wives but none he loved like Bathsheba. It was David's desire to build the temple but he was forbidden by God. This was also part of David's punishment. Solomon would build the temple. David was a mighty conqueror. Though he was a great man of war, he could still be meek and merciful. He was a writer, a poet and a musician.

He is credited with writing the majority of one of the most beloved books in the Bible. The book of Psalms. The twenty third Psalm is probablythe most well known chapters in the Bible. Although we do not know the exact number of Psalms that were written by David. We do know the Psalms were either written for David or about David. David is a type of Christ. Like Christ, he is the good shepherd. Christ was called the son of David. The linage of Christ goes directly back to David, the son of Jesse.

By his successful wars David succeeded in making Israel an independent state and causing his own name to be respected by all the surrounding nations. A notable exploit at the beginning of his reign was the conquest of the Jebusite city of Jerusalem, which he made the capital of his kingdom. It is known as "The City Of David." It is the political center of the nation.

The life of David was an important epoch in the history of Israel. He was the real founder of the monarchy and the head of the dynasty. Chosen by God, "As a man according to his own heart." David was tried in the school of suffering during his days of exile. He developed into a military leader of great renown. To him was due, the complete organization of the army.

David gave Israel a capital, a court, and a great center of religious worship. When he became King of all Israel, there were 339,600 men under his command. At the census 1,300,000 men were enumerated as capable of bearing arms. As a standing army, consisting of twelve corps, each 24,000 men took turns in serving for a month at a time as the garrison of Jerusalem.

King David is one of the most important figures in Jewish history. Born in 907 BCE, he reigns as king of Israel for 40 years, dying at age 70 in 837 BCE. There is so much that can be said about King David. Some people like to focus on the warrior aspect. He was a chivalrous warrior fighting for God. But when his persona and accomplishments are considered as a whole, it is his spiritual greatness that shines most of all.

The very name David means, "Beloved." From the time he was a child, David went with a prayer or song of praise in his heart and is credited with writing some of the most precious Psalms. Even today we as Christians, often look to the book of Psalms for comfort and praise. The good shepherd will always leave the ninety and nine, to find that one sheep which is lost.

The good shepherd will sacrifice his own life, to save that of his beloved sheep. David was always about the business of the father. He tended the sheep for both his earthly father and his heavenly father, always showing and proving the greatest of love. Many legends have grown around the figure of David.

According to Rabbinic tradition, David was raised as the illegitimate son of his father Jesse and spent his early years herding his father's sheep, while his older brothers were in school. There is one thing we know for certain, David was the little shepherd boy... Who would become one of Israel's greatest kings.

About Moses

ACCORDING to the Book of Exodus, Moses was born in a time when his people, the Children of Israel, were increasing in number and the Egyptian Pharaoh was worried that they might help Egypt's enemies. Moses' Hebrew mother, Jochebed, hid him when the Pharaoh ordered all newborn Hebrew boys to be killed, and the child was adopted as a foundling by the Egyptian royal family. After killing an Egyptian slave-master, Moses fled across the Red Sea to Midian where he encountered the God of Israel in the form of a "burning bush". God sent Moses to request the release of the Israelites. After the Ten Plagues, Moses led the Exodus of the Israelites out of Egypt and across the Red Sea, after which they based themselves at Mount

Sinai, where Moses received the Ten Commandments. After 40 years of wandering in the desert, Moses died within sight of the Promised Land.

In the Hebrew Bible, the narratives of Moses are in Exodus, Leviticus, Numbers and Deuteronomy. According to the Book of Exodus, Moses was a son of Amram, a member of the Levite tribe of Israel descended from Jacob, and his wife, Jochebed. Jochebed (also Yocheved) was kin to Amram's father Kehath (Exodus 6:20). Moses had one older (by seven years) sister, Miriam, and one older (by three years) brother, Aaron. According to Genesis 46:11, Amram's father Kehath immigrated to Egypt with 70 of Jacob's household, making Moses part of the second generation of Israelites born during their time in Egypt.

In the Exodus account, the birth of Moses occurred at a time when an unnamed Egyptian Pharaoh had commanded that all male Hebrew children born be killed by drowning in the river Nile. Jochebed, the wife of the Levite Amram, bore a son and kept him concealed for three months. When she could keep him hidden no longer, rather than deliver him to be killed, she set him adrift on the Nile River in a small craft of bulrushes coated in pitch. Moses' sister Miriam observed the progress of the tiny boat until it reached a place where Pharaoh's daughter (Bithiah, Thermuthis) was bathing with her handmaidens. It is said that she spotted the baby in the basket and had her handmaiden fetch it for her. Miriam came forward and asked Pharaoh's daughter if she would like a Hebrew woman to nurse the baby. Thereafter, Jochebed was employed as the child's nurse. He grew up and was brought to Pharaoh's daughter and became her son and a younger brother to the future Pharaoh of Egypt. Moses would not be able to become Pharaoh because he was not the 'blood' son of Bithiah, and he was the youngest.

Shepherd in Midian

After Moses had reached adulthood, he saw an Egyptian beating a Hebrew. Moses killed the Egyptian and buried his body in the sand. Moses soon discovered that the affair was known, and that Pharaoh was likely to put him to death for it; he then fled from Egypt across the Sinai Peninsula. In Midian he stopped at a well where he protected seven shepherdesses from a band of rude shepherds. The shepherdesses' father Hobab adopted him as his son. Hobab gave his daughter Zipporah to Moses in marriage, and made him the superintendent of his herds. Moses lived in Midian for forty years as a shepherd, during which time his son Gershom was born. One day, Moses led his flock to Mount Horeb (Exodus 3), usually identified with Mount Sinai — a mountain that was thought in the Middle Ages to be located on the Sinai Peninsula. There he saw a bush that burned, but was not consumed. When Moses came to look more closely, God spoke to him from the bush, revealing his name to Moses.

Egypt: the Plagues and the Exodus

God commanded Moses to go to Egypt and deliver his fellow Hebrews from bondage. On the way Moses was nearly killed by God because his son was not circumcised. He was met on the way by his elder brother, Aaron, and gained a hearing with his oppressed kindred after they returned to Egypt, who believed Moses and Aaron after they saw the signs that were performed in the midst of the Israelite assembly. Moses and Aaron went to Pharaoh and told him that the Lord God of Israel wanted Pharaoh to permit the Israelites to celebrate a feast in the wilderness. Pharaoh replied that he did not know their God and would not permit them to go. They gained a second hearing with Pharaoh and changed Moses' rod into a serpent, but Pharaoh's magicians did the same with their rods. Moses and Aaron met Pharaoh at the Nile riverbank, and Moses had Aaron turn the river to blood, but Pharaoh's magicians could do the same. Moses obtained a fourth meeting, and had Aaron bring frogs from the Nile to overrun Egypt, but Pharaoh's magicians were able to do the same thing. Pharaoh asked Moses to remove the frogs and promised to let the Israelites go observe their feast in the wilderness in return. Pharaoh decided against letting the Israelites leave to observe the feast.[Eventually Pharaoh let the Hebrews depart after Moses' God sent ten plagues upon the Egyptians. The third and fourth were the plague of gnats and flies. The fifth was diseases on the Egyptians' cattle, oxen, goats, sheep, camels, and horses. The sixth was boils on the skins of Egyptians. Seventh, fiery hail and thunder. The eighth plague was locusts. The ninth plague was total darkness. The tenth plague was the slaying of the Egyptian male first-born children, whereupon such terror seized the Egyptians that they ordered the Hebrews to leave. The events are commemorated as Passover, referring to how the plague "passed over" the houses of the Israelites while smiting the Egyptians.

The crossing of the Red Sea

Main article: *The Exodus*

Moses then led his people eastward, beginning the long journey to Canaan. The procession moved slowly, and found it necessary to encamp three times before passing the Egyptian frontier — some believe at the Great Bitter Lake, while others propose sites as far south as the northern tip of the Red Sea. Meanwhile, Pharaoh had a change of heart, and was in pursuit of them with a large army. Shut in between this army and the sea, the Israelites despaired, but Exodus records that God divided the waters so that they passed safely across on dry ground. There is some contention about this passage, since an earlier incorrect translation of *Yam Suph* to Red Sea was later found to have meant Reed Sea. When the Egyptian army attempted to follow, God permitted the waters to return upon them and drown them.

The people then continued to Marsa marching for three days along the wilderness of the Shur without finding water. Then they came to Elim where twelve water springs and 70 Palm trees greeted them. From Elim they set out again and after 45 days they reached the wilderness of Sin between Elim and Sinai.

From there they reached the plain of Rephidim, completing the crossing of the Red Sea.

Mount Sinai and the Ten Commandments

Main article: Ten Commandments

According to the Bible, after crossing the Red Sea and leading the Israelites towards the desert, Moses was summoned by God to Mount Sinai, also referred to as Mount Horeb, the same place where Moses had first talked to the Burning Bush, tended the flocks of Jethro his father-in-law, and later produced water by striking the rock with his staff and directed the battle with the Amalekites.

Moses stayed on the mountain for 40 days and nights, a period in which he received the Ten Commandments directly from God. Moses then descended from the mountain with intent to deliver the commandments to the people, but upon his arrival he saw that the people were involved in the sin of the Golden Calf. In terrible anger, Moses broke the commandment tablets and ordered his own tribe (the Levites) to go through the camp and kill everyone, including family and friends, upon which the Levites killed about 3,000 people, some of whom were children. God later commanded Moses to inscribe two other tablets, to replace the ones Moses smashed, so Moses went to the mountain again, for another period of 40 days and nights, and when he returned, the commandments were finally given.

In Jewish tradition, Moses is referred to as "The Lawgiver" for this singular achievement of delivering the Ten Commandments.

The years in the wilderness

A statue of Moses smiting the rock stands in Washington Park, Albany, New York.

When the people arrived at Marah, the water was bitter, causing the people to murmur against Moses. Moses cast a tree into the water, and the water became sweet. Later in the journey the people began running low on supplies and again murmured against Moses and Aaron and said they would have preferred to die in Egypt, but God's provision of manna from the sky in the morning and quail in the evening took care of the situation. When the people camped in Rephidim, there was no water, so the people complained again and said, "Wherefore is this that thou hast brought us up out of Egypt, to kill us and our children and our cattle with thirst?" Moses struck a rock with his staff, and water came forth.

Amalekites arrived and attacked the Israelites. In response, Moses bade Joshua lead the men to fight while he stood on a hill with the rod of God in his hand. As long as Moses held the rod up, Israel dominated the fighting, but if Moses let down his hands, the tide of the battle turned in favor of the Amalekites. Because Moses was getting tired, Aaron and Hur had Moses sit on a rock. Aaron held up one arm, Hur held up the other arm, and the Israelites routed the Amalekites.

Jethro, Moses' father-in-law, came to see Moses and brought Moses' wife and two sons with him. After Moses had told Jethro how the Israelites had escaped Egypt, Jethro went to offer sacrifices to the Lord, and then ate bread with the elders. The next day Jethro observed how Moses sat from morning to night giving judgement for the people. Jethro suggested that

Moses appoint judges for lesser matters, a suggestion Moses heeded.

When the Israelites came to Sinai, they pitched camp near the mountain. Moses commanded the people not to touch the mountain. Moses received the Ten Commandments orally (but not yet in tablet form) and other moral laws. He then went up with Aaron, Nadab, Abihu, and seventy of the elders to see the god of Israel. Before Moses went up the mountain to receive the tablets, he told the elders to direct any questions that arose to Aaron or Hur. While Moses was on Mount Sinai receiving instruction on the laws for the Israelite community, the Israelites went to Aaron and asked him to make gods for them. After Aaron had received golden earrings from the people, he made a golden calf and said, "These are your gods, O Israel, who brought you up out of Egypt." A "solemnity of the Lord" was proclaimed for the following day, which began in the morning with sacrifices and was followed by revelry.

After Moses had persuaded the Lord not to destroy the people of Israel, he went down from the mountain and was met by Joshua. Moses destroyed the calf and rebuked Aaron for the sin he had brought upon the people. Seeing that the people were uncontrollable, Moses went to the entry of the camp and said, "Who is on the Lord's side? Let him come unto me." All the sons of Levi rallied around Moses, who ordered them to go from gate to gate slaying the idolators.

Following this, according to the last chapters of *Exodus*, the Tabernacle was constructed, the priestly law ordained, the plan of encampment arranged both for the Levites and the non-priestly tribes, and the Tabernacle consecrated. Moses was given eight prayer laws that were to be carried out in regards to the Tabernacle. These laws included light, incense and sacrifice.

Miriam and Aaron spoke against Moses on account of his marriage to an Ethiopian, Josephus explains the marriage of Moses to this Ethiopian in the *Antiquities of the Jews* and about him being the only one through whom the Lord spoke. Miriam was punished with leprosy for seven days.

The people left Hazeroth and pitched camp in the wilderness of Paran. (Paran is a vaguely defined region in the northern part of the Sinai peninsula, just south of Canaan) Moses sent twelve spies into Canaan as scouts, including most famously Caleb and Joshua. After forty days, they returned to the Israelite camp, bringing back grapes and other produce as samples of the regions fertility. Although all the spies agreed that the land's resources were spectacular, only two of the twelve spies (Joshua and Caleb) were willing to try to conquer it, and are nearly stoned for their unpopular opinion. The people began weeping and wanted to return to Egypt. Moses turned down the opportunity to have the Israelites completely destroyed and a great nation made from his own offspring, and instead he told the people that they would wander the wilderness for forty years until all those twenty years or older who had refused to enter Canaan had died, and that their children would then enter and possess Canaan. Early the next morning, the Israelites said they had sinned and now wanted to take possession of Canaan. Moses told them not to attempt it, but the Israelites chose to disobey Moses and invade Canaan, but were repulsed by the Amalekites and Canaanites.

The Tribe of Reuben, led by Korah, Dathan, Abiram, and 250 Israelite princes accused Moses and Aaron of raising themselves over the rest of the people. Moses told them to come the next morning with a censer for every man. Dathan and Abiram refused to come when summoned by Moses. Moses went to the place of Dathan and Abiram's tents. After Moses spoke the ground opened up and engulfed Dathan and Abiram's tents, after which it closed again. Fire consumed the 250 men with the censers. Moses had the censers taken and made into plates to cover the altar. The following day, the Israelites came and accused Moses and Aaron of having killed his fellow Israelites. The people were struck with a plague that killed 14,700 persons, and was only ended when Aaron went with his censer into the midst of the people. To prevent further murmurings and settle the matter permanently, Moses had each of the chief princes of the non-Levitic tribes write his name on his staff and had them lay them in the sanctuary. He also had Aaron write his name on his staff and had it placed in the tabernacle. The next day, when Moses went into the tabernacle, Aaron's staff had budded, blossomed, and yielded almonds.

After leaving Sinai, the Israelites camped in Kadesh. After more complaints from the Israelites, Moses struck the stone twice, and water gushed forth. However, because Moses and Aaron had not shown the Lord's holiness, they were not permitted to enter the land to be given to the Israelites This was the second occasion Moses struck a rock to bring forth water; however, it appears that both sites were named Meribah after these two incidents.

Moses lifts up the brass serpent, curing the Israelites from poisonous snake bites in a painting by Benjamin West.

Now ready to enter Canaan, the Israelites abandoned the idea of attacking the Canaanites head-on in Hebron, a city in the southern part of Canaan. Having been informed by spies that they were too strong, it was decided that they would flank Hebron by going further East, around the Dead Sea. This required that they pass through Edom, Moab, and Ammon. These three tribes were considered Hebrews by the Israelites as descendants of Lot, and therefore could not be attacked. However they were also rivals, and did not therefore give permission to allow the Israelites to pass openly through their territory. So Moses lead his people carefully along the eastern border of Edom, the southernmost of these territories. While the Israelites were making their journey around Edom, they complained about the *manna*. After many of the people had been bitten by serpents and died, Moses made the brass serpent and mounted it on a pole, and if those who were bitten looked at it, they did not die According to the Biblical Book of Kings this brass serpent remained in existence until the days of King Hezekiah, who destroyed it after persons began treating it as an idol When they reached Moab, it was revealed that Moab had been attacked and defeated by the Amorites led by a king named Sihon. The Amorites were a non-Hebrew Canaanic people who once held power in the Fertile Crescent. When Moses asked the Amorites for passage and it was refused, Moses attacked the Amorites (as non-Hebrews, the Israelites had no reservations in attacking them), presumably weakened by conflict with the Moabites, and defeated them The Israelites, now holding the territory of the Amorites just north of Moab, desired to expand their holdings by acquiring Bashan, a fertile territory north of Ammon famous for its oak trees and cattle. It was led by a king named Og. Later rabbinical legends made Og a survivor of the flood, suggesting the he had sat on the Ark and was fed by Noah. The Israelites fought with Og's forces at Edrei, on the southern border of Bashan, where the Israelites were victorious and slew every man, woman, and child of his cities and took spoil for their bounty.

Balak, king of Moab, having heard of the Israelites' conquests, feared that his territory might be next. Therefore he sent elders of Moab, and of Midian, to Balaam (apparently a powerful and respected prophet), son of Beor (Bible), to induce him to come and curse the Israelites. Balaam's location is unclear. Balaam sent back word that he could only do what God commands, and God has, via a dream, told him not to go. Moab consequently sent higher ranking priests and offers Balaam honours, and so God tells Balaam to go with them. Balaam thus set out with two servants to go to Balak, but an Angel tried to prevent him. At first the Angel is seen only by the ass Balaam is riding. After Balaam started to punish the ass for refusing to move, it is miraculously given the power to speak to Balaam, and it complains about Balaam's treatment. At this point, Balaam was allowed to see the angel, who informed him that the ass is the only reason the Angel did not kill Balaam. Balaam immediately repented, but is told to go on.

Balak met with Balaam at Kirjath-huzoth, and they went to the high places of Baal, and offered sacrifices at seven altars, leading to Balaam being given a prophecy by God, which Balaam relates to Balak. However, the prophecy blesses Israel; Balak remonstrated, but Balaam reminded him that he can only speak the words put in his mouth, so Balak took him to another high place at Pisgah, to try again. Building another seven altars here, and making sacrifices on each, Balaam provided another prophecy blessing Israel. Balaam was finally taken by a now very frustrated Balak to Peor, and, after the seven sacrifices there, decided not to seek enchantments but instead looked on the Israelites from the peak. The spirit of God came upon Balaam and he delivered a third positive prophecy concerning Israel. Balak's anger rose to the point where he threatened Balaam, but Balaam merely offered a prediction of fate. Balaam then looked on the Kenites, and Amalekites and offered two more predictions of fate. Balak and Balaam then go to their respective homes. Later, Balaam informed Balak and the Midianites that, if they wished to overcome the Israelites for a short interval, they needed to seduce the Israelites to engage in idolatry. The Midianites sent beautiful women to the Israelite camp to seduce the young men to partake in idolatry, and the attempt proved successful.

God then commanded Moses to kill and hang the heads of everyone who had engaged in idolatry, and Moses ordered the judges to carry out the mass execution. At the same time, one of the Israelites brought home a Midianitish woman in the sight of the congregation. Upon seeing this, Phinehas, the grandson of Aaron, took a javelin in his hand and thrust through both the Israelite and the Midianitish woman, which turned away the wrath of God. By that time, however, the plague inflicted on the Israelites had already killed about twenty-four thousand persons. Moses was then told that because Phinehas had averted the wrath of God from the Israelites, Phinehas and his descendents were given the pledge of an everlasting priesthood. After Moses had taken a census of the people, he sent an army to avenge the perceived evil brought on the Israelites by the Midianites. Numbers 31 says Moses instructed the Israelite soldiers to kill every Midianite woman, boy, and non-virgin girl, although virgin girls were shared amongst the soldiers. The Israelites killed Balaam, and the five kings of Midian: Evi, Rekem, Zur, Hur, and Reba.

Moses appointed Joshua, son of Nun, to succeed him as the leader of the Israelites. Moses then died at the age of 120.

Death

Moses was warned that he would not be permitted to lead the Israelites across the Jordan river, because of his trespass at the waters of Meribah (Deut. 32:51) but would die on its eastern shores (Num. 20:12). He therefore assembled the tribes, and delivered to them a parting address, which is taken to form the Book of Deuteronomy.

When Moses finished, he sang a song and pronounced a blessing on the people. He then went up Mount Nebo to the top of Pisgah, looked over the promised land of Israel spread out before him, and died, at the age of one hundred and twenty, according to Talmudic legend on 7 Adar, his 120th birthday exactly. God Himself buried him in an unknown grave in a valley in the land of Moab, over against Bethpeor (Deut. 34:6).

Moses was thus the human instrument in the creation of the nation of Israel by communicating to it the Torah. More humble than any other man (Num. 12:3), he enjoyed unique privileges, for "there hath not arisen a prophet since in Israel like unto Moses, whom YHWH knew face to face" (Deut. 34:10). See also Jude 1:9 and Zechariah 3.

Mosaic law

Further information: Law of Moses, Mosaic authorship, Deuteronomist, Book_of_Deuteronomy#Deuteronomic code, and 613 Mitzvot

The Book of Kings relates how a "law of Moses" was discovered in the Temple during the reign of King Josiah (r. 641–609 BC). This book is mostly identified as an early version of the Book of Deuteronomy, perhaps chapters 5-26 and chapter 28 of the extant text. This text contains a number of laws, dated to the 8th century BC kingdom of Judah, a time when a minority Yahwist faction was actively attacking mainstream polytheism, succeeding in establishing official monolatry of the God of Israel under Josiah by the late 7th century BC.

The law attributed to Moses, specifically the laws set out in Deuteronomy, as a consequence came to be considered supreme over all other sources of authority (the king and his officials), and the Levite priests were the guardians and interpreters of the law.

The Book of Deuteronomy (Deuteronomy 31:9 and Deuteronomy 31:24–26) describes how Moses writes "torah" (instruction) on a scroll and lays it beside the Ark of the Covenant. Similar passages include, for example, Exodus 17:14, "And YHWH said unto Moses, Write this for a memorial in a book, and rehearse it in the ears of Joshua, that I will utterly blot out the remembrance of Amalek from under heaven;" Exodus 24:4, "And Moses wrote all the words of YHWH, and rose up early in the morning, and built an altar under the mount, and twelve pillars, according to the twelve tribes of Israel;" Exodus 34:27, "And Yahweh said unto Moses, Write thou these words, for after the tenor of these words I have made a covenant with thee and with Israel;" and Leviticus 26:46 "These are the decrees, the laws and the regulations that the LORD established on Mount Sinai between himself and the Israelites through Moses."

Based on this tradition, "Mosaic law" came to refer to the entire legal content of the Pentateuch, not just the Ten Commandments explicitly connected to Moses in the biblical narrative. The content of this law was excerpted and codified in Rabbinical Judaism as the 613 Mitzvot. By Late Antiquity, the tradition of Moses being the source of the law in the Pentateuch also gave rise to the tradition of Mosaic authorship, the interpretation of the entire Torah as the work of Moses.

Who Was Moses?:

Moses was an early leader of the Hebrews and probably the most important figure in Judaism. He was raised in the court of the Pharaoh in Egypt, but then led the Hebrew people out of Egypt. Moses is said to have talked with God. His story is told in the Bible in the book of *Exodus*.

Moses - Birth & Early Childhood:

The story of Moses' childhood comes from *Exodus*. In it, the pharaoh of Egypt (probably Ramses II) decreed that all the Hebrew boy babies were to be drowned at birth, in a story similar to that of the founder of Rome, Romulus and his twin Remus, and the Sumerian king Sargon I. Yocheved, Moses' mother, hid her newborn for 3 months and then placed her baby in a wicker basket in the Nile River reeds. The baby cried and was rescued by one of the pharaoh's daughters who kept the baby.

Moses and His Mother:

Moses' sister Miriam was watching when the daughter of the pharaoh took the baby. Miriam came forward to ask the princess if she would like a Hebrew wet nurse for the infant. When the princess agreed, Miriam fetched Yocheved.

Moses Commits a Crime:

Moses grew up in the palace as an adopted son of the pharaoh's daughter, but he went to see his own people when he grew up. When he witnessed an overseer beating a Hebrew, he struck the Egyptian and killed him, with the beaten Hebrew as a witness. The pharaoh learned that Moses was the murderer and ordered his execution.

Moses fled to the land of Midian, where he married Tzipporah, daughter of Jethro. Their son was Gershom.

Moses Returns to Egypt:

Moses returned to Egypt to seek the release of the Hebrews and to bring them to Canaan, as a result of God speaking to him in a burning bush. When the pharaoh wouldn't release the Hebrews, Egypt was afflicted with 10 plagues, the last being the killing the firstborn. After this, the pharaoh told Moses he could take the Hebrews. He then reversed his decision and had his men follow Moses into the Red or Reed Sea, which is the scene of one of Moses' miracles - the parting of the Red Sea.

Moses and the Biblical Exodus:

During the 40-year journey of the Hebrews from Egypt to Canaan, Moses received the 10 Commandments from God at Mt. Sinai. While Moses communed with

God for 40 days, his followers built a golden calf. Angry, God wanted to kill them, but Moses dissuaded him. However, when Moses saw the actual shenanigans, he was so angry he hurled and shattered the 2 tablets holding the 10 Commandments.

Moses is Punished and Dies at 120:

It is not clear what exactly Moses did to receive punishment (see Comment From Reader), but God tells Moses that he failed to trust Him sufficiently and for that reason Moses would never enter Canaan. Moses climbed Mt. Abarim to see Canaan, but that was about as close as he came. Moses chose Joshua as successor. At the ripe old age of 120, Moses climbed Mt. Nebo and died after the Hebrews entered the promised land.

Horned Moses:

Moses is sometimes shown with horns coming out of his head. A knowledge of Hebrew would help here since the word "horned" appears to be an alternate translation of the "shiny" appearance Moses exhibited after he came down Mt. Sinai following his tete-a-tete with God in Exodus 34.

Comments:

- **On the Punishment of Moses** It is in Numbers 20:6-11. God tells Moses to speak to the rock, and water will come from it. Instead, Moses goes beyond what the Lord actually asks him to do. (Verses 10-11) In addition to speaking to the rock Moses 1) chastises the people, 2) drew attention to himself – "we" – rather than God, and 3) struck the rock, rather than merely speaking to it. And Moses did fail to trust completely and it is suggested that Moses did not think a mere word was sufficient to produce the water. He felt he must also do something; strike the rock." - Rachel Davison

About Joseph (son of Jacob)

Joseph in the Bible – The Joseph of the Old Testament

ONE JOSEPH IN the Bible was the overconfident younger son of Jacob. He was known to his older brothers as their father's favorite. For this reason his 10 older brothers conspired against the boy and sold him to slave traders, while telling their father the boy had been mauled by an animal. Joseph had been given dreams of God's plan for his life; so with confidence and strength, he endured in this amazing story in Genesis.

The slave traders took him into Egypt and sold him to Potiphar, one of the Pharaoh's officers. Joseph served his master well and gained great favor. But the master's wife tried to seduce Joseph, a young man of impeccable integrity. After he rejected her, she went to her husband with false accusations. It resulted in Joseph's imprisonment. Once again, God proved his presence and protection for Joseph. The prison keeper befriended him and learned of Joseph's divine ability to interpret dreams.

Because of earning this reputation, Joseph was called upon to interpret a dream that deeply troubled the Pharaoh. None of the Pharaoh's wise consults had been able to decipher the dream. But Joseph accurately relayed the symbols in the dream to a future time of abundance that would be followed by a time of great famine. The Pharaoh rewarded Joseph with overseeing the lands of Egypt. In these prosperous times he stored up the abundant harvest toward the tragic times ahead. During the years of famine, Joseph's brothers came in search of grains and foods to keep their people from starvation. Not recognizing their young Hebrew brother as this matured and prominent Egyptian, he ordered them to return with their younger brother. When the brothers returned with Benjamin, Joseph revealed his identity. The brother's suffered from great remorse of their actions and Joseph forgave them. It was a joyous reunion between a grieved father and lost son. Joseph's years of steadfast reliance on God brought about not only reunion but his high position so that he was able to save a nation from starvation.

— YOU CAN'T KEEP A GOOD MAN DOWN

Joseph, son of Jacob and Rachel, was one of the great heroes of the Old Testament. Despite the jealousy of his brothers and some very bad luck, Joseph triumphed. He had a high opinion of himself and did not know when to keep his mouth shut, but he also had superlative administrative skills, quick intelligence and the ability to impress the right people. In other words, a man who was bound to succeed.

JOSEPH AS A BOY

Joseph was the elder son of Jacob's favorite wife Rachel. He seems to have been Jacob's favorite son too. From an early age he showed promise. He was clever, sensible, trustworthy. But he was also spoiled and cosseted, so that his brothers became furiously jealous of the favor he was shown. One example of this cosseting was the long-sleeved coat his father gave Joseph - a coat designed so that the wearer could not do any heavy work. This meant his brothers had to carry Joseph's share of the work as well as their own, and they could not have been happy about this. He also told tales about them to their father, and got them into trouble.

Joseph had dreams, and he was always interested in the meaning of these dreams. Twice he dreamt that he dominated his whole family, including his father and mother. Unfortunately he did not keep quiet about these dreams, but shared them with his brothers, who became increasingly irritated by what they saw as his conceit and arrogance.

One day his father Jacob sent Joseph to check on his brothers who were in the fields shepherding their flocks. The brothers saw him coming in the distance, and before he had reached them they had determined to kill him. Reuben, the eldest, tried to head them off. He was successful insofar as they did not kill Joseph, but instead threw him down into an empty water cistern.

Then the brothers sat down to eat, but as they ate they saw a caravan of camels approaching. Judah, another of the brothers, suggested they sell Joseph to these traders, instead of killing him - he was, after all, their brother. This was what they did. They sold their young brother for twenty pieces of silver, the going rate for a male slave. To cover up what they had done, they killed a goat and smeared its blood on Joseph's coat. Then they took it to Jacob and told him Joseph had been killed by a wild beast. Jacob was distraught, and could not be comforted at the loss of his beloved son.

JOSEPH AS A SLAVE IN EGYPT

The traders had taken Joseph to Egypt, where they sold him to a wealthy official called Potiphar. It was a good buy, Potiphar found. Joseph had great talent as an administrator, and soon rose to a position of importance in the household. He was so good at what he did that quite soon Potiphar was able to leave the running of his estates to Joseph, and divert himself with other pleasures - notably, food.

Joseph was young, clever and handsome. Potiphar had a wife who was rich, bored and lonely. Before long, the inevitable happened. She fell violently in love with Joseph, and could think of nothing else but him - the Egyptians had a frank and uninhibited interest in sexual love, as their poetry shows.

'Lie with me', she said.

Joseph was in a dilemma: he could not betray his master, but he could not avoid his master's wife. One day she cornered him and pulled the loose cloak off his body, leaving him naked. He ran away, but she was furious at the rebuff - a woman scorned. So she shouted 'Rape!' and told the other members of the household that Joseph had attacked her. She pointed to the cloak as proof.

When her husband came home, she told him the same story. He was enraged, and had Joseph put in prison. (For more on the story of Potiphar's wife, see BIBLE WOMEN: POTIPHAR'S WIFE)

But even in prison Joseph prospered. The jailer saw how capable Joseph was, and entrusted the prisoners to him.

One day she cornered him and pulled the loose cloak off his body, leaving him naked. He ran away, but she was furious at the rebuff - she was a woman scorned. So she shouted 'Rape!

JOSEPH AS A PRISONER

Now Joseph administered the prison, and while doing so he made friends with some of the prisoners. Among them were two important officials, Pharaoh's cup-bearer and his baker. They had each had a strange dream, and Joseph was able to successful interpret their dreams, telling the men what was about to happen to them. One of them was freed and restored to his former position. The other was sentenced to death and executed. Joseph had been right about the future of each man.

Two years later Pharaoh himself had a dream, and asked his wisest men to interpret it. They could not. Then the cupbearer remembered Joseph, and told Pharaoh about this Hebrew man who could interpret dreams. Pharaoh sent for Joseph and told Joseph the dream he had had. Joseph immediately knew what it meant, and told Pharaoh. It was a warning of a famine that was soon to happen. But there would be seven good years first, giving Pharaoh time to prepare stores of food for the seven bad harvests that would follow.

Pharaoh was impressed by Joseph's interpretation, and believed it. He decided to organize food storage on a grand scale, and looked round for someone who could supervise this immense task. His eye fell on Joseph, who was given the task. They would collect all the surplus from the good years and keep it in reserve against the seven years of famine that were to follow.

Pharaoh took off his signet ring and gave it to Joseph. Now only Pharaoh was more powerful than Joseph.

JOSEPH AND HIS BROTHERS REUNITED

The seven good years followed, and then came the seven years of famine, just as Joseph had predicted. It hit not only Egypt, but Israel as well. Joseph's family were affected as much as the Egyptian were, and Jacob sent the ten older brothers down into Egypt to see if they could find grain there.

Unknown to them, Joseph was now in charge of selling grain, and when he saw them he recognized them immediately. They did not recognize him.

He was not friendly to them, accusing them of being spies come to reconnoiter the land. They groveled, insisting on their innocence. He repeated the accusations, and put them in prison. Only if they brought the youngest brother, who had been left at home with Jacob, would he believe them. He harried and tormented them before he finally revealed his identity - and then he wept so loudly that Pharaoh was informed of what was happening.

The reconciliation was complete. They sent for their father Jacob, who hardly believe his son Joseph was still alive. Jacob came to Egypt, reunited with the son he had loved so much, and met Joseph's two sons Ephraim and Manasseh.

It was a wonderful moment. He spoke to all his children, told them he wished to be buried in the filed that Abraham had bought as a burial site for his descendants. Then he 'drew up his feet into the bed, breathed his last, and was gathered to his people'. Joseph was overcome with grief. He had had so little time with his father. Then he had his father's body embalmed, and he and a great company of relatives and servants accompanied the body on the journey.

When Jacob had been buried, Joseph and his brothers all moved back to Egypt, where they settled, and where eventually Joseph died.

About Paul

SAUL (PAUL) was born around the same time as Christ. His given name was Saul and later he would be called Paul. Paul was a citizen of the capital city of Cilicia, Tarsus. This country was a Roman land located along the river Cydnus. Tarsus was home to a university and Saul while young received the best education possible. Saul's father was of the tribe of Benjamin, pure and unmixed was his Jewish blood and he was molded it what one would interpret from his youth to adulthood in a staunch and upright character.

"Acts 23:6 But when Paul perceived that the one part were Sadducees, and the other Pharisees, he cried out in the council, Men and brethren, I am a Pharisee, the son of a Pharisee: of the hope and resurrection of the dead I am called in question."

"Philippians 3:5-6 Circumcised the eighth day of the stock of Israel, of the tribe of Benjamin, an Hebrew of the Hebrews; as touching the law, a Pharisee; 6 Concerning zeal, persecuting the church; touching the righteousness which is in the law, blameless."

Paul was sent to the Jewish school of learning at Jerusalem to study law. He was around 13 when he began his studies under the well-known Gamaliel. Gamaliel was a rabbi and very educated. After his studies he returned to Tarsus but soon after the death of Christ he returned to Jerusalem where Christianity was becoming wide-spread. It seemed that through out Jerusalem and the outskirt areas Christianity was becoming very popular. Saul was a key player in what was to take place in the life of the Christians and he became very active in the part of persecuting the Christians. Although Paul had never met Jesus he became first a vital part of the persecution of the Christians and then became a very vital player in the spreading of the Gospel of Christ to the nations.

Paul was on the Damascus road to carrying a list of suspected Christians when something happened to him. On the Damascus road Saul was converted and this conversion changed the course of his life and the Christian faith. The journey that Saul was on with the list of names of Christians was a long journey and would take Saul around 7 days. Saul was on the road with his attendants when he was struck blind on the road and fell before the living Lord. A brilliant light shone bright and Saul heard a voice saying,

"Acts 9:4 "¦ Saul, Saul, why persecutest thou me? 5 And he said, Who art thou, Lord? And the Lord said, I am Jesus whom thou persecutest: it is hard for thee to kick against the pricks. 6 And he trembling and astonished said, Lord, what wilt thou have me to do? And the Lord said unto him, Arise, and go into the city, and it shall be told thee what thou must do."

Saul, now baptized Paul by Ananais was taken from the city for his safety to Arabia where he lived for a short time. Soon though Paul visited Jerusalem staying with Peter and James, Jesus' brother. Paul was approached by Barnabas a friend from Jerusalem to help the church of Antioch. Paul and Barnabas began traveling together preaching the Gospel of Christ. Paul's preaching aroused the tempers of the Jewish leaders and he was quickly opposed by both the Jewish and Christian communities. Paul insisted that the only requirement to be a Christian was to be saved through Jesus Christ, and not saved by keeping the law of man.

Paul against the warnings of others insisted on going to Jerusalem where he was captured and put in prison. Paul spent a little more than two years in prison without a trial and was finally granted a hearing before the Emperor of Rome. At this hearing Paul was finally released but soon arrested again. It is believed that it was shortly after this arrest that Paul was beheaded. It is thought that the beheading took place most probably around 66 A.D. four years before Jerusalem fell. Most all of Paul's writings were done during his times of imprisonment. His true love for the Christ he never physically met is a shining example for all believers today.

Paul's writings consisted of letters to the churches and a large percentage of the New Testament is credited to Paul. Paul's writings are as follows: Romans, 1st & 2nd Corinthians, Galatians, Ephesians, Philippians, Colossians, 1st & 2nd Thessalonians, 1st & 2nd Timothy, Titus, Philemon

Paul the Apostle (c. AD 5 – c. AD 67; also known as "the Apostle Paul", "Saint Paul" and "Saul of Tarsus") is perhaps the most influential early Christian missionary and leader of the first generation of Christians. Among the many other apostles and missionaries involved in the spread of the Christian faith, Paul is often considered to be one of the two most important people in the history of Christianity, and one of the greatest religious leaders of all time. Almost half of the books of the New Testament are credited to his authorship. He was responsible for spreading of the Gospel through early Christian communities across the Roman Empire. From the mid-30s to the mid-50s he established several churches in Asia Minor and at least three in Europe, including the church at Corinth.

According to writings in the book of Acts,[7:58-13:9] [22:7] [26:14] Paul grew up in Jerusalem, and his Jewish name was "Saul", the name of Israel's first king. "Paul" was the apostle's Latin name.

For the first half of his life, he was a member of the Pharisees, a Jewish faction that promoted orthodoxy and formalism. They were formidable persecutors of the new Christian movement. Paul's persecutions likely involved traveling from synagogue to synagogue and urging the punishment of Jews who accepted Jesus as the messiah. While traveling on the road from Jerusalem to Damascus on a mission to "bring these people as prisoners to Jerusalem to be punished",[Acts 22:5] the resurrected Jesus appeared to him in a great light. He was struck blind, but after three days his sight was restored by Ananias of Damascus, and Paul began to preach that Jesus of Nazareth is the Jewish Messiah and the Son of God.[Acts 9:20-21]

He never claimed to be innovative in his doctrine or ideas. Instead, he saw himself as an ambassador for Jesus who carried out the directives and teachings of his Lord (cf. 2 Cor. 5:18-20). Paul was compelled to struggle to validate his own worth and authority. His contemporaries probably did not hold him in esteem as high as they held Peter and James. Along with Simon Peter and James the Just he was one of the most prominent early Christian leaders.

Thirteen epistles in the New Testament are traditionally attributed to Paul. More than half of the book of Acts is devoted to describing his pioneering activities. Augustine of Hippo developed Paul's idea that salvation is based on faith and not "works of the law". Martin Luther's interpretation of Paul's writings heavily influenced Luther's doctrine of sola fide. His writings' influence on Christian thinking has been significant, due in part to his association as a prominent apostle of Christianity during the spreading of the Gospel through early Christian communities across the Roman Empire.

The book of Acts contains many more details about Paul's early life than appear in his letters. He was a native of Tarsus, the capital city of Cilicia. Acts 21:39 He grew up in Jerusalem where he studied "at the feet of Gamaliel", a famous rabbi at the time. Acts 22:3

Paul's conversion dramatically changed the course of his life. Through his missionary activity and writings he eventually transformed religious belief and philosophy around the Mediterranean Basin. His leadership, influence and legacy led to the formation of communities dominated by Gentile groups that worshiped the God of Israel, adhered to the "Judaic moral code", but relaxed or abandoned the ritual and dietary teachings of the Law of Moses, that these laws and rituals had either been fulfilled in the life of Christ or were symbolic precursors of Christ, all on the basis of Paul's teachings of the life and works of Jesus Christ and his teaching of a New Covenant (or "new testament")[Heb. 9:15] established through Jesus' death and resurrection.

The Bible does not record Paul's death. In his second letter to Timothy, Paul writes about anticipating his death. Writing around 110, Ignatius noted that Paul had been martyred.

Conversion of Saint Paul, a fresco by Michelangelo.

The main source for information about Paul's life is the material found in his epistles and the book of Acts. However, these epistles contain comparatively little information about Paul's past. The book of Acts also recounts Paul's career but leaves several parts of Paul's life out of its narrative, such as his (alleged) execution in Rome. Scholars such as Hans Conzelmann and 20th century theologian John Knox dispute the historical reliability of the Acts of the Apostles. Paul's own account of his background is found particularly in Galatians. According to some scholars, the *Acts* account of Paul visiting Jerusalem[Acts 11:27–30] contradicts the account in Paul's letters.[16] Some scholars consider Paul's accounts to be more reliable than those found in Acts.

Sources outside of the New Testament that mention Paul include:

His given name was Saul (Hebrew: שָׁאוּל, Modern Sha'ul Tiberian Šāʾûl ; "asked for, prayed for"), perhaps after the biblical King Saul, a fellow Benjamite and the first king of Israel. In biblical Greek: Σαούλ (Saul), Σαῦλος (Saulos), and Παῦλος (Paulos). And in Latin: Saul, Saulus and Paulus.

In the book of Acts, when he had the vision that led to his conversion on the Road to Damascus, Jesus called him "Saul, Saul" in the Hebrew tongue, and later, in a vision to Ananias of Damascus, "the Lord" referred to him as "Saul of Tarsus".[Acts 9:11] When Ananias came to restore his sight, he called him "Brother Saul".[Acts 9:17;22:13]

In Acts 13:9, the author indicates a name change by saying, "...Saul, (who also is called Paul,)..." and thereafter refers to him as Paul. He is called Paul in all other Bible books where he is mentioned. Mark Powell concludes that "Saul/Paul seems to have had two names: his given Hebrew name ('Saul') and a more Roman-sounding name ('Paul') for use in the Gentile world (similarly, Silus was called 'Silvanus')".

Early life

Paul was a Greek-speaking Jew from Asia Minor. He was born in Tarsus which was a major city in eastern Cilicia, a region that had become part of the Roman province of Syria by the time of his adulthood. Damascus and Antioch, two of the main cities in Syria.

It is inferred that he was born about the same time as Jesus (c. 4 B.C.) or slightly later. He was converted to faith in Jesus Christ about A.D. 33. He died c. A.D. 62-64, most likely in Rome.

His father was a Roman citizen.[Acts 22:26-28] [cf. Acts 16:37] The family had a history of piety.[2 Timothy 1:3] Apparently the family lineage had been very attached to Pharisaic traditions and observances for generations. [Philippians 3:5-6] Young Saul learned how to make the mohair with which tents were made. [Acts 18:1-3] Later as a Christian missionary, that trade became a means of support for him, one that he could practice anywhere. It also was to become an initial connection with Priscilla and Aquila with whom he would partner in tent-making and later become very important teammates as fellow missionaries.

When he was still very young, he was sent to Jerusalem to receive his education at the school of Gamaliel,[Acts 22:3] apparently a very distinguished and well-known Jewish teacher. Some of his family may have resided in the holy city since later there is mention of the presence of one of his sisters whose son saved his life.[Acts 23:16] Absolutely nothing more is known of his background until he takes an active part in the martyrdom of Stephen.[Acts 7:58-60;22:20] At that point he could have been between twenty and forty.[25]

Prior to conversion

Paul claimed to be "of the stock of Israel, of the tribe of Benjamin, a Hebrew of the Hebrews; as touching the law, a Pharisee."[Phil. 3:5] But the Bible reveals very little about Paul's family. Paul's "sister's son" is mentioned in Acts 23:16. *Acts* also quotes Paul indirectly referring to his father by saying he was "a Pharisee, the son of a Pharisee".[Acts 23:6] Paul refers to his mother in Romans 16:13 as among those at Rome.

Acts identifies Paul as from the Mediterranean city of Tarsus (in present-day south-central Turkey), well known for its intellectual environment.[Acts 21:39]

Although born in Tarsus, Paul was raised in Jerusalem[Acts 26:4] "at the feet of Gamaliel",[Acts 22:3] a leading authority in the Sanhedrin in the mid-1st century A.D. Gamaliel once gave some advice to the Sanhedrin to "refrain" from slaying the disciples of Jesus.[Acts 5:34–39] This is in great contrast to the rashness of his student Saul, who zealously persecuted the "saints".[Acts 9:13;26:10]

Paul confesses that "beyond measure" he persecuted the "church of God" prior to his conversion.[Gal. 1:13–14] [Phil. 3:6] [Acts 8:1-3] As a young man, he cooperated in the killing of the proto-martyr, Stephen, standing by and guarding the clothes of the witnesses while Stephen was stoned.[Acts 7:58; 8:1; 22:20]

His "Damascus Road experience"

Geography relevant to Paul's life, stretching from Jerusalem to Rome

Paul's conversion can be dated to 31–36[26][27][28] by his reference to it in one of his letters.[12] There are three accounts of his conversion (or metanoia) in the Acts of the Apostles: Acts 9:1–31, 22:1–22, and 26:9–24.

It took place on the road to Damascus where he reported to have experienced a vision of the resurrected Jesus. The account in Acts 9 says that both Saul/Paul and the men that were with him heard the voice asking, "Saul! Saul! Why are you persecuting me?" Saul asked,

"Who are you, lord?", to which the voice replied, "I am Jesus, the one you are persecuting! Now get up and go into the city, and you will be told what you must do." From that experience he was blinded for three days and had to be led into Damascus by the hand. His sight was restored by Ananias of Damascus. This profound experience and revelation convinced Paul that God indeed had chosen Jesus to be the promised messiah. Luke, the author of Acts of the Apostles, likely learned of his conversion from Paul, from the church in Jerusalem, or from the church in Antioch.[29]

Post-conversion change of heart and mind

In the opening verses of Romans 1, Paul provides a litany of his own apostolic appointment to preach among the Gentiles[Gal. 1:16] and his post-conversion convictions about the risen Christ.

- Paul described himself as

    a servant of Christ Jesus
    called to be an apostle
    set apart for the gospel of God

- Paul described Jesus as

    having been promised by God "beforehand" through his prophets in the holy Scriptures being the true messiah and the Son of God having biological lineage from David ("according to the flesh") having been declared to be the Son of God in power according to the Spirit of holiness by his resurrection from the dead being Jesus Christ our Lord the One through whom we have received grace and apostleship to bring about the obedience of faith for the sake of his name among all the nations, "including you who are called to belong to Jesus Christ."

- Jesus

    lives in heaven
    is God's Son
    would soon return

- The Cross

    he had believed death by crucifixion was a shameful sign that signified being cursed by God now believed Jesus' death was a voluntary sacrifice that reconciled sinners with God[Rom. 5:6-10] [Phil. 2:8]

- The Law

    he had believed the law (Jewish Torah) kept people in a right relationship with God[Gal. 2:16] [Gal. 3:12] now believed the law only reveals the extent of people's enslavement to the power of sin—a power that must be broken by Christ[Rom. 3:20b][7:7-12]

- Gentiles

he had believed Gentiles were outside the covenant that God made with Israel now he believed Gentiles and Jews were united as the people of God in Christ Jesus[Gal. 3:28]

- Circumcision

had believed circumcision was the rite through which males became part of Israel, an exclusive community of God's chosen people[Phil. 3:3-5] now believed baptism was the rite through which people became part of the church—an inclusive community of Jews and Gentiles reconciled with God through faith[Rom. 6:4]

- Persecution

had believed his violent persecution of the church to be an indication of his zeal for his religion[Phil. 3:6] now believed Jewish hostility toward the church was sinful opposition that would incur God's wrath[1 Thess. 2:14-16]:p.236

- The Last Days

    had believed God's messiah would put an end
    to the old age of evil and initiate a new age of
    righteousness now believed this would happen
    in stages that had begun with the resurrection
    of Jesus, but the old age would continue until
    Jesus returns[Rom. 16:25] [1 Cor. 10:11] [Gal.
    1:4][5]:p.236

Early ministry

The house believed to be of Ananias of Damascus
in Damascus

Bab Kisan, believed to be where Paul escaped from
persecution in Damascus

After his conversion, Paul went to Damascus, where
Acts states he was healed of his blindness and
baptized by Ananias of Damascus. Paul says that it
was in Damascus that he barely escaped death. [2
Cor. 11:32] Paul also says that he then went first to
Arabia, and then came back to Damascus.[Gal. 1:17]
Paul's trip to Arabia is not mentioned anywhere else
in the Bible, and some suppose he actually traveled to
Mt. Sinai for meditations in the desert. He describes
in Galatians how three years after his conversion he
went to Jerusalem. There he met James and stayed
with Simon Peter for 15 days.[Gal. 1:13–24] Afterwards,

Paul proclaims that Mount Sinai is located in Arabia. [Gal. 4:24-25]

Paul asserted that he received the Gospel not from an apostle, but directly by the revelation of Jesus Christ. [Gal. 1:11-12] Paul claimed almost total independence from the Jerusalem community and yet appeared eager to bring material support to Jerusalem from the various budding Gentile churches that he planted. In his writings, Paul persistently used the persecutions he claimed to have endured, in terms of physical beatings and verbal assaults, to claim proximity and union with Jesus and as a validation of his teaching.

Paul's narrative in Galatians states that 14 years after his conversion he went again to Jerusalem. [Gal. 2:1-10] It is not completely known what happened during these 'unknown years', but both Acts and Galatians provide some partial details. At the end of this time, Barnabas went to find Paul and brought him back to Antioch. [Acts 11:26]

When a famine occurred in Judea, around 45-46, Paul and Barnabas journeyed to Jerusalem to deliver financial support from the Antioch community. According to Acts, Antioch had become an alternative center for Christians following the dispersion of the believers after the death of Stephen. It was in Antioch that the followers of Jesus were first called "Christians." [Acts 11:26]

First missionary journey

The author of the Acts arranges Paul's travels into three separate journeys. The first journey,[Acts 13-14] led initially by Barnabas, takes Paul from Antioch to Cyprus then southern Asia Minor (Anatolia), and back to Antioch. In Cyprus, Paul rebukes and blinds Elymas the magician[Acts 13:8-12] who was criticizing their teachings. From this point on, Paul is described as the leader of the group.

They sail to Perga in Pamphylia. John Mark leaves them and returns to Jerusalem. Paul and Barnabas go on to Pisidian Antioch. On Sabbath they go to the synagogue. The leaders invite them to speak. Paul reviews Israelite history from life in Egypt to King David. He introduces Jesus as a descendant of David brought to Israel by God. He said that his team came to town to bring the message of salvation. He recounts the story of Jesus' death and resurrection. He quotes from the Septuagint to assert that Jesus was the promised Christos who brought them forgiveness for their sins. Both the Jews and the 'God-fearing' Gentiles invited them to talk more next Sabbath. At that time almost the whole city gathered. This upset some influential Jews who spoke against them. Paul used the occasion to announce a change in his mission which from then on would be to the Gentiles.[Acts 13:13-48]

Antioch served as a major Christian center for Paul's evangelizing.

Second missionary journey

Saint Paul delivering the *Areopagus sermon* in Athens, by Raphael, 1515. This sermon addressed early issues in Christology.

Paul leaves for his second missionary journey from Jerusalem, in late Autumn after the meeting of the Council of Jerusalem where the circumcision question was debated. On their trip around the Mediterranean Sea, Paul and his companion Barnabas stopped in Antioch where they had a sharp argument about taking John Mark with them on their trips. The book of Acts said that John Mark had left them in a previous trip and gone home. Unable to resolve the dispute, Paul and Barnabas decided to separate; Barnabas took John Mark with him, while Silas joined Paul.

Paul and Silas initially visited Tarsus (Paul's birthplace), Derbe and Lystra. In Lystra, they met Timothy, a disciple who was spoken well of, and decided to take him with them. The Church kept growing, adding believers, and strengthening their faith daily. [Acts 16:5]

In Philippi, certain men were not happy about the liberation of their soothsaying servant girl, who had been possessed with a spirit of divination,[Acts 16:16–24] and they turned the city against the missionaries and Paul and Silas were put in jail. After a miraculous earthquake, the gates of the prison fell apart and Paul and Silas were able to escape but remained; this event led to the conversion of the jailor.[Acts 16:25-40] They continued traveling, going by Berea and then to Athens where Paul preached to the Jews and God-fearing Greeks in the synagogue and to the Greek intellectuals in the Areopagus.

Around 50–52, Paul spent 18 months in Corinth. The reference in Acts to proconsul Gallio helps ascertain this date (cf. Gallio inscription). In Corinth, Paul met Aquila and Priscilla who became faithful believers and helped Paul through his other missionary journeys. The couple followed Paul and his companions to Ephesus, and stayed there to start one of the strongest and most faithful churches at that time. In 52, the missionaries sailed to Caesarea to greet the Church there and then traveled north to Antioch where they stayed for about a year before leaving again on their third missionary journey.

Third missionary journey

Paul began his third missionary journey by traveling all around the region of Galatia and Phrygia to strengthen, teach and rebuke the believers. Paul then traveled to Ephesus, an important center of early Christianity, and stayed there for almost three years. He performed numerous miracles, healing people and casting out demons, and he apparently organized missionary activity into the hinterlands. Paul left Ephesus after an attack from a local silversmith resulted in a pro-Artemis riot involving most of the city. During his stay in Ephesus, Paul wrote four letters to the church in Corinth admonishing them for their pagan behavior.

Paul went through Macedonia into Achaea and made ready to continue on to Syria, but he changed his plans and traveled back through Macedonia because of Jews who had made a plot against him. At this time, it is likely that Paul visited Corinth for three months. In Romans 15:19 Paul wrote that he visited Illyricum, but he may have meant what would now be called Illyria Graeca, which lay in the northern part of modern Albania, but was at that time a division of the Roman province of Macedonia.

Paul and his companions visited other cities on their way back to Jerusalem such as Philippi, Troas, Miletus, Rhodes, and Tyre. Paul finished his trip with a stop in Caesarea where he and his companions stayed with Philip the Evangelist before finally arriving at Jerusalem. [Acts 21:8–10] [21:15]

Journey to Rome and beyond

After Paul's arrival in Jerusalem at the end of his third missionary journey, he became involved in a serious conflict with some "Asian Jews" (most likely from

Roman Asia). The conflict eventually led to Paul's arrest and imprisonment in Caesarea for about a year and a half. Finally, Paul and his companions sailed for Rome where Paul was to stand trial for his alleged crimes. *Acts* states that Paul preached in Rome for two years from his rented home while awaiting trial. It does not state what happened after this time, but some sources claim that Paul was freed by Nero and continued to preach in Rome even though that seems unlikely based on Nero's historical relationship with Early Christians. It is possible that Paul also traveled to other countries like Spain and Britain. See the *Arrest and death* section below.

Among the writings of early Christians, Clement of Rome said that Paul was "Herald (of the Gospel of Christ) in the West," and that "he had gone to the extremity of the west." Chrysostom indicated that Paul preached in Spain: "For after he had been in Rome, he returned to Spain, but whether he came thence again into these parts, we know not." Cyril of Jerusalem said that Paul, "fully preached the Gospel, and instructed even imperial Rome, and carried the earnestness of his preaching as far as Spain, undergoing conflicts innumerable, and performing Signs and wonders". The Muratorian fragment mentions "the departure of Paul from the city [of Rome] when he journeyed to Spain."

Council of Jerusalem

Main article: Council of Jerusalem

See also: Circumcision controversy in early Christianity

Most scholars agree that a vital meeting between Paul and the Jerusalem church took place some time in the years 48 to 50, described in Acts 15:2 and usually seen as the same event mentioned by Paul in Galatians 2:1. The key question raised was whether Gentile converts needed to be circumcised. At this meeting, Paul claims in his letter to the Galatians that Peter, James, and John accepted Paul's mission to the Gentiles.

Jerusalem meetings are mentioned in Acts, in Paul's letters, and some appear in both. For example, the Jerusalem visit for famine relief[Acts 11:27–30] apparently corresponds to the "first visit" (to Cephas and James only).[Gal. 1:18–20] F. F. Bruce suggested that the "fourteen years" could be from Paul's conversion rather than from his first visit to Jerusalem.

Incident at Antioch

Main article: Incident at Antioch

Despite the agreement achieved at the Council of Jerusalem, as understood by Paul, Paul recounts how he later publicly confronted Peter in a dispute sometimes called the "Incident at Antioch," over

Peter's reluctance to share a meal with Gentile Christians in Antioch because they did not strictly adhere to Jewish customs.

Writing later of the incident, Paul recounts, "I opposed [Peter] to his face, because he was clearly in the wrong," and says he told Peter, "You are a Jew, yet you live like a Gentile and not like a Jew. How is it, then, that you force Gentiles to follow Jewish customs?"[Gal. 2:11–14] Paul also mentions that even Barnabas, his traveling companion and fellow apostle until that time, sided with Peter.

The final outcome of the incident remains uncertain. The Catholic Encyclopedia suggests that Paul won the argument, because "Paul's account of the incident leaves no doubt that Peter saw the justice of the rebuke." L. Michael White's *From Jesus to Christianity* draws the opposite conclusion: "The blowup with Peter was a total failure of political bravado, and Paul soon left Antioch as persona non grata, never again to return."

The primary source account of the Incident at Antioch is Paul's letter to the Galatians.

Visits to Jerusalem in Acts and the epistles

This table is adapted from White, *From Jesus to Christianity*. Note that the matching of Paul's travels in the Acts and the travels in his Epistles is done for the reader's convenience and is not approved of by all scholars.

Arrest and death

Paul arrived in Jerusalem with a collection of money for the community there. Acts reports that he was warmly received. But Acts goes on to recount how Paul was warned by James and the elders that he was gaining a reputation for being against the Law, 'teaching all the Jews living among the gentiles to forsake Moses, and that you tell them not to circumcise their children or observe the customs'.[Acts 21:21] Paul underwent a purification ritual in order to give the Jews no grounds to bring accusations against him for not following their law. Paul caused a stir when he appeared at the Temple, and he escaped being killed by the crowd by being taken into Roman custody. When a plot to kill Paul on his way to an appearance before the Jews was discovered, he was transported by night to Caesarea. He was held as a prisoner there for two years, until a new governor reopened his case in 59. When the governor suggested that he be sent back to Jerusalem for further trial, Paul was constrained to "appeal unto Caesar", as was his right as a Roman.

Acts recounts that on the way to Rome, Paul was shipwrecked on "Melita" (Malta),[Acts 28:1] where he was met by Publius[Acts 28:7] and the islanders who showed him "unusual kindness".[Acts 28:2] He arrived in Rome c. 60 and spent two years under house arrest. [Acts 28:16]

Irenaeus of Lyons in the 2nd century believed that Peter and Paul had been the founders of the Church in Rome and had appointed Linus as succeeding bishop. Paul was not a bishop of Rome nor did he bring Christianity to Rome since there were already Christians in Rome when he arrived there.[Acts 28:14–15] Also, Paul wrote his letter to the church at Rome before he had visited Rome.[Romans 1:1,7,11-13;15:23–29] However, Paul would have played an important role in the life of the early church at Rome.

Neither the Bible nor other sources say how or when Paul died, but Ignatius, probably around 110, writes that Paul was martyred. Christian tradition holds that Paul was beheaded in Rome during the reign of Nero around the mid-60s at *Tre Fontane Abbey* (English: Three Fountains Abbey). By comparison, tradition states that Peter, who was not a Roman citizen, was given the more painful death of being crucified upside-down.

In June 2009, Pope Benedict announced excavation results concerning the tomb of Paul at the Basilica of Saint Paul Outside the Walls. The sarcophagus was not opened but was examined by means of a probe, which revealed pieces of incense, purple and blue linen, and small bone fragments. The bone was radiocarbon dated to the 1st or 2nd century. According to the Vatican, these findings are consistent with the traditional claim that the tomb is Paul's. The sarcophagus was inscribed in Latin saying, "Paul apostle martyr."

Writings

Main article: *Pauline Epistles*

Of the 27 books in the New Testament, 13 are attributed to Paul, and approximately half of another, the Book of Acts, deals with Paul's life and works. Paul provides the first written account of what it is to be a Christian and thus a description of Christian spirituality. His letters have been characterized as being the most influential books of the New Testament after the Gospels of Matthew and John.

Paul...only occasionally had the opportunity to revisit his churches. He tried to keep up his converts' spirit, answer their questions, and resolve their problems by letter and by sending one or more of his assistants (especially Timothy and Titus). Paul's letters reveal a remarkable human being: dedicated, compassionate, emotional, sometimes harsh and angry, clever and quick-witted, supple in argumentation, and above all possessing a soaring, passionate commitment to God, Jesus Christ, and his own mission. Fortunately, after his death one of his followers collected some of the letters, edited them very slightly, and published them. They constitute one of history's most remarkable personal contributions to religious thought and practice.

Basic message

- His strongest emphasis was on the death, resurrection, and lordship of Jesus Christ. He preached that one's faith in Jesus assures that person a share in Jesus' life (salvation). He saw Jesus' death as being for the believers' benefit, not a defeat. Jesus died so that believers' sins will be purged.

- The resurrection of Jesus was of primary importance to Paul as may be seen in his letter to the Thessalonians[1 Thes. 1:9-10]—the earliest surviving account of conversion to the Christian movement.

- The resurrection brought the promise of salvation to believers. Paul taught that those who died in Christ would be raised when Christ returned, while those still alive would be "caught up in the clouds together with them to meet the Lord in the air".[1 Thes. 4:14-18]

Sanders concludes that these and many other passages reveal what he calls the essence of the Christian message:

1. God sent his Son

2. The Son was crucified for the benefit of humanity

3. The Son would soon return

4. Those who belonged to the Son would live with him forever

5. Followers are to live by the highest moral standard—"May your spirit and soul and body be kept sound and blameless at the coming of our Lord Jesus Christ."[1 Thes. 5:23]

Paul…only occasionally had the opportunity to revisit his churches. He tried to keep up his converts' spirit, answer their questions, and resolve their problems by letter and by sending one or more of his assistants (especially Timothy and Titus). Paul's letters reveal a remarkable human being: dedicated, compassionate, emotional, sometimes harsh and angry, clever and quick-witted, supple in argumentation, and above all possessing a soaring, passionate commitment to God, Jesus Christ, and his own mission. Fortunately, after his death one of his followers collected some of the letters, edited them very slightly, and published them. They constitute one of history's most remarkable personal contributions to religious thought and practice.

He argued that Gentile converts did not need to become Jews, get circumcised, follow Jewish dietary restrictions, or otherwise observe Mosaic laws.

Nevertheless, in Romans he insisted on the positive value of the Law, as a moral guide.

E. P. Sanders' publications have since been taken up by Professor James Dunn who coined the phrase "The New Perspective on Paul". N.T. Wright, the Anglican Bishop of Durham, notes a difference in emphasis between Galatians and Romans, the latter being much more positive about the continuing covenant between God and his ancient people than the former. Wright also contends that performing Christian works is not insignificant but rather proof of having attained the redemption of Jesus Christ by grace (free gift received by faith).[Rom. 2:13ff] He concludes that Paul distinguishes between performing Christian works which are signs of ethnic identity and others which are a sign of obedience to Christ.

World to come

See also: Christian eschatology, Second Coming, End times, and World to Come

According to Ehrman, Paul believed that Jesus would return within his lifetime. He states that Paul expected that Christians who had died in the mean time would be resurrected to share in God's kingdom, and he believed that the saved would be transformed, assuming supernatural bodies.

Paul's teaching about the end of the world is expressed most clearly in his letters to the Christians at Thessalonica. Heavily persecuted, it appears that they had written asking him first about those who had died already, and, secondly, when they should expect the end. He assures them that the dead will rise first and be followed by those left alive.[1 Thes. 4:16ff] This suggests an imminence of the end but he is unspecific about times and seasons, and encourages his hearers to expect a delay. The form of the end will be a battle between Jesus and the man of lawlessness[2 Thess. 2:3] whose conclusion is the triumph of Christ.

Role of women

Main article: Paul the Apostle and women

See also: 1 Timothy 2:12 ("I suffer not a woman")

The second chapter of the first letter to Timothy—one of the six disputed letters—is used by many churches to deny women a vote in church affairs, reject women from serving as teachers of adult Bible classes, prevent them from serving as missionaries, and generally disenfranchise women from the duties and privileges of church leadership.

1 Timothy 2:9 In like manner also, that women adorn themselves in modest apparel, with shamefacedness and sobriety; not with broided hair, or gold, or pearls, or costly array; 10 But (which becometh women

professing godliness) with good works.11 Let the woman learn in silence with all subjection.12 But I suffer not a woman to teach, nor to usurp authority over the man, but to be in silence.13 For Adam was first formed, then Eve.

About Daniel

DANIEL The Prophet From The Bible

Daniel was a young man of deep convictions. He knew and understood the ways of God, even in his youth. He must have spent much of his young life studying the law because he knew it well by the time he was taken captive into Babylon. Daniel knew the importance of remaining pure and undefiled, even in a culture that was saturated with pagan practices and idol worship. It was because of his love for God and his commitment to purity that God entrusted Daniel with the ability to understand and interpret dreams and visions. And this divine ability served him well many times during Daniel's service to the king.

Daniel was among the Israelites taken captive from Jerusalem when King Nebuchadnezzar of Babylon besieged it. Although Scripture does not specifically state so, many scholars believe that Daniel became a eunuch. Yet despite the unfair circumstances, his faith remained strong. Daniel was selected to be part of the king's court because he met certain criteria according to the king's request. The men chosen were to be ones *"in whom there was no blemish, but good-looking, gifted in all wisdom, possessing knowledge and quick to understand, who had ability to serve in the king's palace."* (Daniel 1:4)

Daniel, even as a youth, displayed these characteristics. He already was considered one of the best of the best. But because of Daniel's obedient and submissive heart, God took him and made him better. In fact, the Bible says that in wisdom and understanding, Daniel and his three friends, Shadrach, Meshac, and Abed-nego, were 10 times better than any of the magicians and astrologers in the entire empire.

Daniel's new life in a foreign land included instruction in both the language and literature of the Babylonians. As a eunuch in the king's court, Daniel was exposed daily to the riches, the luxury, and all the other seductions of the Babylonian Empire. Yet he was determined to remain consecrated, not partaking of the delicacies provided to him by the king. To refuse the provisions meant sure consequences for him and for those overseeing his instruction. Yet Daniel remained steadfast, knowing that God would honor his choice to obey divine law rather than the laws of men.

Daniel had a greater respect for and fear of God than he did of the king. Knowing and believing that God would use him, Daniel kept his focus on God. In both the Babylon and the Persian Empires, Daniel was made great in the eyes of the kings and fellow men. The supernatural miracles that occurred in Daniel's life were recognized as ones that only the God of heaven and earth could do. To have the ability to not only interpret a dream but to state the dream without having prior foreknowledge, or to interpret the writings on the wall made by the finger of God, or to be rescued from the mouths of lions, are all displays of the faith of a man who, from his youth, determined to learn and follow the ways of God.

Daniel (Hebrew: דָּנִיֵּאל, Modern Daniyyel Tiberian Dāniyyêl ; Arabic: دانيال, meaning in Hebrew "God is my Judge") is the protagonist in the Book of Daniel of the Hebrew Bible. In the narrative, when Daniel was a young man, he was taken into Babylonian captivity where he was educated in Chaldean thought. However, he never converted to Neo-Babylonian ways. By Divine Wisdom from his God, Yahweh, he interpreted dreams and visions of kings, thus becoming a prominent figure in the court of Babylon. Eventually, he had apocalyptic visions of his own that have been interpreted as the Four monarchies. Some of the most famous accounts of Daniel are: Shadrach, Meshach, and Abednego, The writing on the wall and Daniel in the lions' den.

Induction into Babylon

Daniel refusing to eat at the King's table, early 1900s Bible illustration

In the third year of the reign of Jehoiakim (606 BC), Daniel and his friends Hananiah, Mishael, and Azariah were among the young Jewish nobility carried off to Babylon. The four were chosen for their intellect and beauty to be trained as advisors to the Babylonian court (Daniel 1), Daniel was given the name *Belteshazzar*, i.e., *prince of Bel*, or *Bel protect the king!* (not to be confused with the neo-Babylonian king, Belshazzar). Hananiah, Mishael, and Azariah were given the Babylonian names, Shadrach, Meshach, and Abednego, respectively.

Daniel and Nebuchadnezzar

Main article: Daniel 2

See also: Nebuchadnezzar II#Portrayal in the books of Daniel and Jeremiah and Book of Daniel#Nebuchadnezzar or Nabonidus

In the narrative of Daniel chapter 2, it is the second year of the reign of Nebuchadnezzar and the king is distressed by his dreams.[v.1] Thus he summons his interpreters,[v.2] however, they are unable to relay or interpret the dreams.[v.10-11] The King acts in fury and demands the execution of all the wise men in Babylon. [v.12] When Daniel discovers the King's executive order, he requests from the *captain of the guard*, Arioch, to see the King.[v.13-16] Daniel prays for God's mercy to receive a revelation from the King's dream.[v.15-18] God then reveals the mystery to Daniel in a vision that night.[v.19] Daniel praises his God with a doxology.[v.20-23] After meeting with Arioch again, Daniel is granted access to the king[v.24-30] and relays the description of the dream,[v.31-36] followed by its interpretation. [v.37-45] With Daniel's successful interpretation of the dream, the king expresses homage,[v.46] followed by his own doxology that affirms that Daniel's *God is God of gods* for revealing this *mystery* of his dream.[v.47] Daniel is then promoted as chief governor over the whole province of Babylon.[v.48] At Daniel's request, his companions are also promoted, thus they remain at the king's court.

Nebuchadnezzar's madness

Nebuchadnezzar recounts a dream of a huge tree which is suddenly cut down at the command of a heavenly messenger. Daniel is summoned and interprets the dream. The tree is Nebuchadnezzar himself, who for seven years will lose his mind and become like a wild beast. All of this comes to pass until, at the end of the specified time, Nebuchadnezzar acknowledges that "heaven rules" and his kingdom and sanity are restored and his kingdom is restored to him.

Daniel and Belshazzar

Main article: The writing on the wall

See also: Belshazzar#Belshazzar in literature

In Daniel's later years, king Belshazzar holds a great feast for all his nobles. In a drunken state, the king calls for the sacred vessels captured from the Jerusalem temple and blasphemously drinks from them. Suddenly, the fingers of a man's hand appear before the king and write on the wall of the palace. When none of his wise men are able to interpret the message, Daniel is called in at the suggestion of the queen-mother. After reprimanding the king for his impiety, Daniel interprets the handwriting on the wall to mean that Belzhazzar is about to lose his kingdom to the Medes and the Persians. For successfully reading the cryptic handwriting, Daniel is rewarded with a purple robe and elevated to the rank of "third ruler" of the kingdom. "That very night", we are told, "Belshazzar, king of the Babylonians, was slain" and his successor was King Darius the Mede, aged 62.

Daniel in the Lion's den protected by an angel by François Verdier

Daniel and Darius the Mede

Main article: *Daniel in the lions' den*

See also: *Book of Daniel#Historicity of Darius the Mede*

After the Persian conquest of Babylon, Daniel is depicted as one of three senior administrators of the empire in the reign of Darius the Mede. When the king decides to set Daniel over the whole kingdom, the other officials plot his downfall. Unable to uncover any corruption, they use Daniel's religious devotion to defeat him. The officials trick the king into issuing an irrevocable decree that no god is to be worshiped for a thirty day period. When Daniel continues to pray three times a day towards Jerusalem, he is thrown into a lions den,much to the distress of Darius. After an angel shuts the lions' mouths, Daniel is delivered and the corrupt officials and their wives and children thrown into the den where they are eaten instantly.

Daniel's visions

Main article: *Four monarchies*

Further information: *Daniel 7*, *Daniel 8*, *and* *Daniel 11*

See also: *Prophecy of seventy weeks*

Daniel's ministry as a prophet began late in life. Whereas his early exploits were a matter of common knowledge within his community, these same events, with his pious reputation, serve as the basis for his prophetic ministry. The recognition for his prophetic message is that of other prophets like Isaiah, Jeremiah and Ezekiel whose backgrounds are the basis for their revelations.

From Chapter 7 to the end of the book of Daniel, an apocalyptic vision is being described, supposedly from the perspective of Daniel. This marks a change in the narrative from Daniel interpreting to messengers of God interpreting for Daniel. Daniel dreams of four beasts that come out of the sea: a lion with eagles wings, a bear with three tusks, a leopard with four wings and four heads, and a beast with iron teeth, ten horns and one little horn and human eyes.(Daniel 7:4-8) These beasts are all present at a convening of the divine counsel. Presiding over the counsel is the Ancient of Days, which may, in fact, be the Israelite God. The Ancient One proceeds to put to death the beast with the one little horn. (Daniel 7:9-11) Daniel also describes the fates of the other beasts saying that while their dominion was taken away, their lives were prolonged. (Daniel 7:12) This introduction leads into a series of dreams and visions where these events are expressed in greater detail.

Scholars argue that each of these beasts represent an emperor or kingdom that ruled over the Israelites. The vast majority of scholars[citation needed] accept the first as Babylon, the second as Media/Persia, the third as Greece and the 4th as Rome. The feet and toes represent the modern age which will be destroyed at the return of Christ when Christ is set up as head. A small group believes the first being Babylon, then Media, then Persia, and finally the Greeks. The horns of the last beast may be symbolic of the rulers that replaced Alexander the Great upon his death, culminating with the little horn, or Antiochus IV. There are additional details in the text that allude to Antiochus IV, including some form of desecration to the temple (Daniel 11:31) and persecution (Daniel 11:23). The final message of the second half of Daniel is that God will deliver the people from oppression, the latest of which is Antiochus IV.

Daniel's final days

The time and circumstances of Daniel's death have not been recorded. However, tradition maintains that Daniel was still alive in the third year of Cyrus according to the Tanakh (Daniel 10:1). He would have been almost 101 years old at that point, having been brought to Babylon when he was in his teens, more than 80 years previously. Rabbinic sources indicate that he was still alive during the reign of the Persian king Ahasuerus (Babylonian Talmud, Megillah 15a based on Book of Esther 4, 5). Some say he was killed by Haman, the prime minister of Ahasuerus (Targum Sheini on Esther,

4, 11). Many[who?] posit that he possibly died at Susa in Iran. Tradition holds that his tomb is located in Susa at a site known as **Shush-e Daniyal**. Other locations have been claimed as the site of his burial, including Daniel's Tomb in Kirkuk, Iraq, as well as Babylon, Egypt, Tarsus and, notably, Samarkand, which claims a tomb of Daniel (see "The Ruins of Afrasiab" in the Samarkand article), with some traditions suggesting that his remains were removed, perhaps by Tamerlane, from Susa to Samarkand (see, for instance, Itinerary of Benjamin of Tudela, section 153).

About Jesus

Jesus also referred to as **Jesus of Nazareth**, is the central figure of Christianity, whom the teachings of most Christian denominations believe to be the Son of God.

Virtually all scholars of antiquity agree that Jesus existed. While the quest for the historical Jesus has produced little agreement on the historicity of gospel narratives and their theological assertions of his divinity, most scholars agree that Jesus was a Jewish teacher from Galilee in Roman Judea, was baptized by John the Baptist, and was crucified in Jerusalem on the orders of the Roman Prefect, Pontius Pilate.

Scholars have offered various portraits of the historical Jesus, which at times share a number of overlapping attributes, such as the leader of an apocalyptic movement, Messiah, a charismatic healer, a sage and philosopher, or a social reformer who preached of the "Kingdom of God" as a means for personal and egalitarian social transformation. Scholars have correlated the New Testament accounts with non-Christian historical records to arrive at an estimated chronology of Jesus' life.

Christians hold Jesus to be the awaited Messiah of the Old Testament and refer to him as **Jesus Christ** or simply as Christ, a name that is also used secularly. Most Christians believe that Jesus was conceived by the Holy Spirit, born of a virgin, performed miracles, founded the Church, died sacrificially by crucifixion to achieve atonement, rose from the dead, and ascended into heaven, from which he will return. The majority of Christians worship Jesus as the incarnation of God the Son, and the Second Person of the Holy Trinity.[32] A few Christian groups reject Trinitarianism, wholly or partly, as non-scriptural.

In the Bible he is referred to as "Jesus from Nazareth",[Mt 21:11] "Joseph's son",[Lk 4:22] and "Jesus son of Joseph from Nazareth".[Jn 1:45] Before his death and resurrection, his followers may have begun to refer to him as the Messiah—"Christ" in Greek translation,

---

the anointed one. After his death and resurrection, his followers regularly referred to him as both "Lord" and "Messiah".[Ac 2:36] In his writings, Paul variously used both "Christ" and "Son of God". Paul used "Christ" as if were Jesus' name rather than a title. As an example, in Romans 6:4 he wrote "Christ was raised from the dead". He most often referred to Jesus as "Jesus Christ", "Christ Jesus", or "Christ".

In the New Testament, in Luke 1:26–33, the angel Gabriel tells Mary to name her child "Jesus", and in Matthew 1:21 an angel tells Joseph to name the child "Jesus". The statement in Matthew 1:21 "you are to give him the name Jesus, because he will save his people from their sins" associates salvific attributes to the name Jesus in Christian theology.

"Christ" (pron.: /ˈkraɪst/) is derived from the Greek Χριστός (Khrīstos), meaning "the anointed" or "the anointed one", a translation of the Hebrew מָשִׁיחַ (Māšîaḥ), usually transliterated into English as "Messiah" (pron.: /mɨˈsaɪ.ə/). In the Septuagint version of the Hebrew Bible (written well over a century before the time of Jesus), the word "Christ" (Χριστός) was used to translate the Hebrew word "Messiah" (מָשִׁיחַ) into Greek. In Matthew 16:16, the apostle Peter's profession "You are the Christ" identifies Jesus as the Messiah. In postbiblical usage, "Christ" became viewed as a name, one part of "Jesus Christ", but originally it was a title ("Jesus the Anointed").

Chronology

Main article: Chronology of Jesus

Judea and Galilee at the time of Jesus.

Although a few scholars have questioned the existence of Jesus as an actual historical figure, and some early Christian sects denied that Jesus existed as a physical being (see below), most scholars involved with historical Jesus research believe he existed, but that the supernatural claims associated with him cannot be established using documentary and other evidence. As discussed in the sections immediately below, the estimation of the year of death of Jesus places his lifespan around the beginning of the 1st century AD/CE, in the geographic region of Judea.

Roman involvement in Judea began around 63 BC/BCE and by 6 AD/CE Judea had become a Roman province. From 26–37 AD/CE Pontius Pilate was the governor of Roman Judea. In this time period, although Roman Judea was strategically positioned in the Near East, close to Arabia and North Africa, it was not viewed as a critically important province by the Romans. At the time the Romans were highly tolerant of other religions and allowed the local populations such as the Jews to practice their own faiths.

Year of birth

Further information: Anno Domini, Common Era, and Year zero

In the fourth century, Christians in the West began celebrating the birth of Jesus on December 25 by tradition, while those in the East held it on January 6—with the Chronography of 354 illuminated manuscript including an early reference to a Nativity feast. However, the New Testament includes no mention of the date or season of Jesus' birth and there are no other historical records that pertain to it.

Two independent approaches have been used to estimate the year of the birth of Jesus, one involving analysis of the Nativity accounts in the Gospels of Luke and Matthew along with other historical data, and the other working backwards from the estimation of the start of the ministry of Jesus, as also discussed in the next section.

In its Nativity account, the Gospel of Matthew associates the birth of Jesus with the reign of Herod the Great, who is generally believed to have died around 4 BC/BCE. Matthew 2:1 states that: "Jesus was born in Bethlehem of Judaea in the days of Herod the king" and Luke 1:5 mentions the reign of Herod shortly before the birth of Jesus. Luke's gospel also describes the birth as taking place during the first census, which is generally believed to have occurred in 6 AD/CE Most scholars generally assume a date of birth between 6 and 4 BC/BCE. Other scholars assume that Jesus was born sometime between 7 and 2 BC/BCE.

The year of Jesus' birth has also been estimated in a manner that is independent of the Nativity accounts, by using information in the Gospel of John to work backwards from the statement in Luke 3:23 that Jesus was "about 30 years of age" at the start of his ministry. As discussed in the section below, by combining information from John 2:13 and John 2:20 with the writings of Flavius Josephus, it has been estimated that around 27–29 AD/CE, Jesus was "about thirty years of age". Some scholars thus estimate the year 28 AD/CE to be roughly the 32nd birthday of Jesus and the birth year of Jesus to be around 6–4 BC/BCE.

The Gregorian calendar method for numbering years, in which the current year is 2013, is based on the decision the 6th century monk Dionysius to count the years from a point of reference (namely, Jesus' birth) which he placed sometime between 2 BC and 1 AD.

Years of ministry

Main article: Ministry of Jesus

Israel Museum model of Herod's Temple, referred to in John 2:13.

There have been different approaches to estimating the date of the start of the ministry of Jesus. One approach, based on combining information from the Gospel of Luke with historical data about Emperor Tiberius yields a date around 28–29 AD/CE, while a second independent approach based on statements in the Gospel of John along with historical information from Josephus about the Temple in Jerusalem leads to a date around 27–29 AD/CE. A third method uses the date of the death of John the Baptist and the marriage of Herod Antipas to Herodias based on the writings of Josephus, and correlates it to Matthew 14:4.

The estimation of the date based on the Gospel of Luke relies on the statement in Luke 3:1–2 that the ministry of John the Baptist which preceded that of Jesus began "in the fifteenth year of the reign of Tiberius Caesar". Given that Tiberius began his reign in 14 AD/CE, this yields a date about 28–29 AD/CE.

The estimation of the date based on the Gospel of John uses the statements in John 2:13 that Jesus went to the Temple in Jerusalem around the start of his ministry and in John 2:20 that "Forty and six years was this temple in building" at that time. According to Josephus (Ant 15.380) the temple reconstruction was started by Herod the Great in the 15th–18th year of his reign at about the time that Augustus arrived in Syria (Ant 15.354). Temple expansion and reconstruction was ongoing, and it was in constant reconstruction until it was destroyed in 70 AD/CE by the Romans. Given that it took 46 years of construction, the Temple visit in the Gospel of John has been estimated at around 27–29 AD/CE.

Scholars estimates that John the Baptist's imprisonment probably occurred around AD/CE 30–32. The death of John the Baptist relates to the end of the *major Galilean ministry* of Jesus, just before the half way point in the gospel narratives. Luke 3:23 states that at the start of his ministry Jesus was "about 30 years of age". The length of the ministry is subject to debate, based on the fact that the synoptic gospels mention only one passover during Jesus' ministry, often interpreted as implying that the ministry lasted approximately one year, whereas the Gospel of John records multiple passovers, implying that his ministry may have lasted at least three years.

Year of death

Main article: Chronology of Jesus

A 1466 copy of Antiquities of the Jews.

A number of approaches have been used to estimate the year of the death of Jesus, including information from the canonical gospels, the chronology of the life of Paul the Apostle in the New Testament correlated with historical events, as well as different astronomical models, as discussed below.

The 4 gospels report that Jesus was crucified by Pontius Pilate, who governed Roman Judea from 26 to 36 AD/ CE. Jewish historian Josephus, writing in *Antiquities of the Jews* (*c*. 93 AD/CE), and the early 2nd century Roman historian Tacitus, writing in *The Annals* (*c*. 116 AD/CE), also state that Pilate ordered the execution of Jesus.

The estimation of the date of the conversion of Paul places the death of Jesus before this conversion, which is estimated at around 33–36 AD/CE. The estimation of the year of Paul's conversion relies on a series of calculations working backwards from the well established date of his trial before Gallio in Achaea Greece (Acts 18:12–17) around 51–52 AD/CE, the meeting of Priscilla and Aquila which were expelled from Rome about 49 AD/CE and the 14-year period before returning to Jerusalem in Galatians 2:1. The remaining period is generally accounted for by Paul's missions (at times with Barnabas) such as those in Acts 11:25–26 and 2 Corinthians 11:23–33, resulting in the 33–36 AD/CE estimate.

Isaac Newton was one of the first astronomers to estimate the date of the crucifixion and suggested Friday, April 23, 34 AD/CE. In 1990 astronomer Bradley E. Schaefer computed the date as Friday, April 3, 33 AD/CE. In 1991, John Pratt stated that Newton's method was sound, but included a minor error at the end. Pratt suggested the year 33 AD/CE as the answer. Using the completely different approach of a lunar eclipse model, Humphreys and Waddington arrived at the conclusion that Friday, April 3, 33 AD/CE was the date of the crucifixion.

Life and teachings in the New Testament

Main article: Life of Jesus in the New Testament

Although the four canonical gospels, Matthew, Mark, Luke, and John, are the main sources for the biography of Jesus' life, other parts of the New Testament, such as the Pauline epistles which were likely written decades before them, also include references to key episodes in his life such as the Last Supper, as in 1 Corinthians 11:23–26. The Acts of the Apostles (10:37–38 and 19:4) refers to the early ministry of Jesus and its anticipation by John the Baptist. And Acts 1:1–11 says more about the Ascension episode (also mentioned in 1 Timothy 3:16) than the canonical gospels.

According to the majority viewpoint, the Synoptic Gospels are the primary sources of historical information about Jesus and of the religious movement he founded, but not everything contained in the gospels is considered to be historically reliable. Elements whose historical authenticity are disputed include the two accounts of the Nativity of Jesus, as well as the resurrection and certain details about the crucifixion. On one extreme, some Christian scholars maintain that the gospels are inerrant descriptions of the life of Jesus. On the other extreme, some scholars have concluded that the gospels provide no historical information about Jesus' life.

Canonical gospel accounts

A 3rd-century Greek papyrus of Luke.

Three of the four canonical gospels, namely Matthew, Mark, and Luke, are known as the synoptic Gospels, from the Greek σύν (syn "together") and ὄψις (opsis "view"), given that they display a high degree of similarity in content, narrative arrangement, language and paragraph structure. The presentation in the fourth canonical gospel, i.e. John, differs from these three in that it has more of a thematic nature rather than a narrative format. Scholars generally agree that it is impossible to find any direct literary relationship between the synoptic gospels and the Gospel of John.

However, in general, the authors of the New Testament showed little interest in an absolute chronology of Jesus or in synchronizing the episodes of his life with the secular history of the age. The gospels were primarily written as theological documents in the context of early Christianity with the chronological timelines as a secondary consideration. One manifestation of the gospels being theological documents rather than historical chronicles is that they devote about one third of their text to just seven days, namely the last week of the life of Jesus in Jerusalem, referred to as Passion Week.

Although the gospels do not provide enough details to satisfy the demands of modern historians regarding exact dates, it is possible to draw from them a general picture of the life story of Jesus. However, as stated in John 21:25 the gospels do not claim to provide an exhaustive list of the events in the life of Jesus. Since the 2nd century attempts have been made to *harmonize* the gospel accounts into a single narrative; Tatian's Diatesseron perhaps being the first. Although there are differences in specific temporal sequences, and in the parables and miracles listed in each gospel, the flow of the key events such as Baptism, Transfiguration and Crucifixion and interactions with people such as the Apostles are shared among the gospel narratives.

Key elements and the five major milestones

The five major milestones in the gospel narrative of the life of Jesus are his Baptism, Transfiguration, Crucifixion, Resurrection and Ascension. These are usually bracketed by two other episodes: his Nativity at the beginning and the sending of the Holy Spirit at the end. The gospel accounts of the teachings of Jesus are often presented in terms of specific categories involving his "works and words", e.g. his ministry, parables and miracles.

The gospels include a number of discourses by Jesus on specific occasions, e.g. the Sermon on the Mount or the Farewell Discourse, and also include over 30 parables, spread throughout the narrative, often with themes that relate to the sermons. Parables represent a major component of the teachings of Jesus in the gospels, forming approximately one third of his recorded teachings, and John 14:10 positions them as the revelations of God the Father. The gospel episodes that include descriptions of the miracle of Jesus also often include teachings, providing an intertwining of his "words and works" in the gospels.

Main articles: Genealogy of Jesus and Nativity of Jesus

The accounts of the genealogy and Nativity of Jesus in the New Testament appear only in the Gospel of Luke and the Gospel of Matthew. While there are documents outside of the New Testament which are more or less contemporary with Jesus and the gospels, many shed no light on the more biographical aspects of his life and these two gospel accounts remain the main sources of information on the genealogy and Nativity.

Matthew begins his gospel in 1:1 with the genealogy of Jesus, and presents it before the account of the birth of

Jesus, while Luke discusses the genealogy in chapter 3, after the Baptism of Jesus in Luke 3:22 when the voice from Heaven addresses Jesus and identifies him as the Son of God. At that point Luke traces Jesus' ancestry through Adam to God.

The Nativity is a prominent element in the Gospel of Luke. It comprises over 10 percent of the text, and is three times the length of the nativity text in Matthew. Luke's account takes place mostly before the birth of Jesus and centers on Mary, while Matthew's takes place mostly after the birth of Jesus and centers on Joseph. According to Luke and Matthew, Jesus was born to Joseph and Mary, his betrothed, in Bethlehem. Both support the doctrine of the Virgin Birth in which Jesus was miraculously conceived in his mother's womb by the Holy Spirit, when his mother was still a virgin.

In Luke 1:31–38 Mary learns from the angel Gabriel that she will conceive and bear a child called Jesus through the action of the Holy Spirit. When Mary is due to give birth, she and Joseph travel from Nazareth to Joseph's ancestral home in Bethlehem to register in the census of Quirinius. In Luke 2:1–7. Mary gives birth to Jesus and, having found no room for themselves in the inn, places the newborn in a manger. An angel visits the shepherds and sends them to adore the child in Luke 2:22. After presenting Jesus at the Temple, Joseph and Mary return home to Nazareth.

Following his betrothal to Mary, Joseph is troubled in Matthew 1:19–20 because Mary is pregnant, but in the first of Joseph's three dreams an angel assures him not be afraid to take Mary as his wife, because her child was conceived by the Holy Spirit.

In Matthew 1:1–12, the Wise Men or Magi bring gifts to the young Jesus as the King of the Jews. King Herod hears of Jesus' birth, but before the Massacre of the Innocents Joseph is warned by an angel in his dream and the family flees to Egypt, after which they return and settle in Nazareth.

Early life and profession

Main article: Child Jesus

See also: Return of young Jesus to Nazareth

In the Gospels of Luke and Matthew, Jesus' childhood home is identified as the town of Nazareth in Galilee. Joseph, husband of Mary, appears in descriptions of Jesus' childhood and no mention is made of him thereafter. The New Testament books of Matthew, Mark, and Galatians mention Jesus' brothers and sisters, but the Greek word *adelphos* in these verses, has also been translated as brother or kinsman.

In Mark 6:3 Jesus is called a *tekton* (τέκτων in Greek), usually understood to mean carpenter. Matthew 13:55 says he was the son of a *tekton*.[170] *Tekton* has been traditionally translated into English as "carpenter", but it is a rather general word (from the same root that leads to "technical" and "technology") that could cover makers of objects in various materials, even builders.

Beyond the New Testament accounts, the specific association of the profession of Jesus with woodworking is a constant in the traditions of the 1st and 2nd centuries and Justin Martyr (d. ca. 165) wrote that Jesus made yokes and ploughs.

Baptism and temptation

Main articles: Baptism of Jesus, Temptation of Christ, and John the Baptist

Trevisani's depiction of the typical baptismal scene with the sky opening and the Holy Spirit descending as a dove,

In the gospels, the accounts of the Baptism of Jesus are always preceded by information about John the Baptist and his ministry. In these accounts, John was preaching for penance and repentance for the remission of sins and encouraged the giving of alms to the poor (as in Luke 3:11) as he baptized people in the area of the River Jordan around Perea about the time of the commencement of the ministry of Jesus. The Gospel of John (1:28) specifies "Bethany beyond the Jordan", i.e. Bethabara in Perea, when it initially refers to it and later John 3:23 refers to further baptisms in Ænon "because there was much water there".

The four gospels are not the only references to John's ministry around the River Jordan. In Acts 10:37–38, Peter refers to how the ministry of Jesus followed "the baptism which John preached".In the Antiquities of the Jews (18.5.2) 1st century historian Josephus also wrote about John the Baptist and his eventual death in Perea.

In the gospels, John had been foretelling (as in Luke 3:16) of the arrival of a someone "mightier than I". Apostle Paul also refers to this anticipation by John in Acts 19:4. In Matthew 3:14, upon meeting Jesus, the Baptist states: "I need to be baptized by you." However, Jesus perses John to baptize him nonetheless. In the baptismal scene, after Jesus emerges from the water, the sky opens and a voice from Heaven states: "This is my beloved Son with whom I am well pleased". The Holy Spirit then descends upon Jesus as a dove in Matthew 3:13–17, Mark 1:9–11, Luke 3:21–23. In John 1:29–33 rather than a direct narrative, the Baptist bears witness to the episode This is one of two cases in the gospels where a voice from Heaven calls Jesus "Son", the other being in the Transfiguration of Jesus episode.

After the baptism, the synoptic gospels proceed to describe the Temptation of Jesus, but John 1:35–37 narrates the first encounter between Jesus and two of his future disciples, who were then disciples of John the Baptist. In this narrative, the next day the Baptist sees Jesus again and calls him the Lamb of God and the "two disciples heard him speak, and they followed Jesus". The Temptation of Jesus is narrated in the three synoptic gospels after his baptism.

Ministry

A 1923 map of Galilee around 50 AD/CE. Nazareth is towards the center.

Luke 3:23 states that Jesus was "about 30 years of age" at the start of his ministry. The date of the start of his ministry has been estimated at around 27–29 AD/CE, based on independent approaches which combine separate gospel accounts with other historical data. The end of his ministry is estimated to be in the range 30–36 AD/CE.

The gospel accounts place the beginning of Jesus' ministry in the countryside of Judea, near the River Jordan. Jesus' ministry begins with his Baptism by John the Baptist (Matthew 3, Luke 3), and ends with the Last Supper with his disciples (Matthew 26, Luke 22) in Jerusalem. The gospels present John the Baptist's ministry as the precursor to that of Jesus and the Baptism as marking the beginning of Jesus' ministry, after which Jesus travels, preaches and performs miracles.

The *Early Galilean ministry* begins when Jesus goes back to Galilee from the Judaean Desert after rebuffing the temptation of Satan. In this early period Jesus preaches around Galilee and in Matthew 4:18–20 his first disciples encounter him, begin to travel with him and eventually form the core of the early Church. This period includes the Sermon on the Mount, one of the major discourses of Jesus.

The *Major Galilean ministry* which begins in Matthew 8 refers to activities up to the death of John the Baptist. It includes the Calming the storm and a number of other miracles and parables. The *Final Galilean ministry* includes the Feeding the 5000 and Walking on water episodes, both in Matthew 14. The end of this period (as Matthew 16 and Mark 8 end) marks a turning point is the ministry of Jesus with the dual episodes of Confession of Peter and the Transfiguration.

As Jesus travels towards Jerusalem, in the *Later Perean ministry*, about one third the way down from the Sea of Galilee along the Jordan, he returns to the area where he was baptized, and in John 10:40–42. The *Final ministry in Jerusalem* is sometimes called the *Passion Week* and begins with the Jesus' triumphal entry into Jerusalem on Palm Sunday. In that week Jesus drives the money changers from the Temple, and Judas bargains to betray him. This period culminates in the Last Supper, and the Farewell discourse. The accounts of the ministry of Jesus generally end with the Last Supper.

Teachings and preachings

Main articles: Sermon on the Mount *and* Parables of Jesus

See also: Sermon on the Plain, Five Discourses of Matthew, Farewell Discourse, *and* Olivet Discourse

Jesus Christ Pantocrator – ancient mosaic from Hagia Sophia.

In the New Testament the teachings of Jesus are presented in terms of his "words and works". The words of Jesus include a number of sermons, as well as parables that appear throughout the narrative of the synoptic gospels (the Gospel of John includes no parables). The works include the miracles and other acts performed during his ministry Although the canonical gospels are the major source of the teachings of Jesus, the Pauline epistles, which were likely written decades before the gospels, provide some of the earliest written accounts of the teachings of Jesus.

The New Testament does not present the teachings of Jesus as merely his own preachings, but equates the words of Jesus with divine revelation, with John the Baptist stating in John 3:34: "he whom God hath sent speaketh the words of God" and Jesus stating in John 7:16: "My teaching is not mine, but his that sent me" and again re-asserting that in John 14:10: "the words that I say unto you I speak not from myself: but the Father abiding in me doeth his works." In Matthew 11:27 Jesus claims divine knowledge, stating: "No one knows the Son except the Father and no one knows the Father except the Son", asserting the mutual knowledge he has with the Father.

Parables represent a major component of the teachings of Jesus in the gospels, the approximately thirty parables forming about one third of his recorded teachings. The parables may appear within longer sermons, as well as other places within the narrative. Jesus' parables are seemingly simple and memorable stories, often with imagery, and each conveys a teaching which usually relates the physical world to the spiritual world.

The gospel episodes that include descriptions of the miracle of Jesus also often include teachings, providing an intertwining of his "words and works" in the gospels. Many of the miracles in the gospels teach the importance of faith, for instance in Cleansing ten lepers and Daughter of Jairus the beneficiaries are told that they were healed due to their faith.

Proclamation as Christ and Transfiguration

Transfiguration of Jesus depicting him with Elijah, Moses and 3 apostles by Carracci, 1594.

At about the middle of each of the three synoptic gospels, two related episodes mark a turning point in the narrative: the Confession of Peter and the Transfiguration of Jesus. These episodes begin in Caesarea Philippi just north of the Sea of Galilee at the beginning of the final journey to Jerusalem which ends in the Passion and Resurrection of Jesus. These episodes mark the beginnings of the gradual disclosure of the identity of Jesus to his disciples; and his prediction of his own suffering and death.

Peter's Confession begins as a dialogue between Jesus and his disciples in Matthew 16:13, Mark 8:27 and Luke 9:18. Jesus asks his disciples: *But who do you say that I am?* Simon Peter answers him: *You are the Christ, the Son of the living God.* In Matthew 16:17 Jesus blesses Peter for his answer, and states: "flesh and blood hath not revealed it unto thee, but my Father who is in heaven." In blessing Peter, Jesus not only accepts the titles *Christ* and *Son of God* which Peter attributes to him, but declares the proclamation a divine revelation by stating that his Father in Heaven had revealed it to Peter. In this assertion, by endorsing both titles as divine revelation, Jesus unequivocally declares himself to be both Christ and the Son of God.

The account of the Transfiguration of Jesus appears in Matthew 17:1–9, Mark 9:2–8, Luke 9:28–36. Jesus takes Peter and two other apostles with him and goes up to a mountain, which is not named. Once on the mountain, Matthew (17:2) states that Jesus "was transfigured before them; his face shining as the sun, and his garments became white as the light." A bright cloud appears around them, and a voice from the cloud states: "This is my beloved Son, with whom I am well pleased; listen to him". The Transfiguration not only supports the identity of Jesus as the Son of God (as in his Baptism), but the statement "listen to him", identifies him as the messenger and mouth-piece of God.

Final week: betrayal, arrest, trial, and death

The description of the last week of the life of Jesus (often called the Passion week) occupies about one third of the narrative in the canonical gospels. The narrative for that week starts by a description of the final entry into Jerusalem, and ends with his crucifixion.

The Last Supper has been depicted by many artistic masters.

The last week in Jerusalem is the conclusion of the journey which Jesus had started in Galilee through Perea and Judea. Just before the account of the final entry of Jesus into Jerusalem, the Gospel of John includes the Raising of Lazarus episode, which builds the tension between Jesus and the authorities. At the beginning of the week as Jesus enters Jerusalem, he is greeted by the cheering crowds, adding to that tension.

During the week of his "final ministry in Jerusalem", Jesus visits the Temple, and has a conflict with the money changers about their use of the Temple for commercial purposes. This is followed by a debate with the priests and the elder in which his authority is questioned. One of his disciples, Judas Iscariot, decides to betray Jesus for thirty pieces of silver.

Towards the end of the week, Jesus has the Last Supper with his disciples, during which he institutes the Eucharist, and prepares them for his departure in the Farewell Discourse. After the supper, Jesus is betrayed with a kiss while he is in agony in the garden, and is arrested. After his arrest, Jesus is abandoned by most of his disciples, and Peter denies him three times, as Jesus had predicted during the Last Supper.

Jesus is first questioned by the Sanhedrin, and is then tried by Pontius Pilate, the Roman governor of Judea. During these trials Jesus says very little, and is mostly silent. After the scourging of Jesus, and his mocking as the King of the Jews Pilate orders the crucifixion.

Thus the final week that begins with his entry into Jerusalem, concludes with his crucifixion and burial on that Friday, as described in the next 5 sub-sections. The New Testament accounts then describe the resurrection of Jesus three days later, on the Sunday following his death.

Final entry into Jerusalem

Main articles: Triumphal entry into Jerusalem, Cleansing of the Temple, and Bargain of Judas

Matthew 21:5 relates Jesus' entry to Zechariah (9:9): "the King cometh unto thee, meek, and sitting upon an ass." Traditionally, arrival on a donkey signifies peace, while war-waging kings ride horses.

In the four canonical gospels, Jesus' Triumphal entry into Jerusalem takes place at the beginning of the last week of his life, a few days before the Last Supper, marking the beginning of the Passion narrative. While at Bethany Jesus sent two disciples to retrieve a donkey that had been tied up but never ridden and rode it into Jerusalem, with Mark and John stating Sunday, Matthew Monday, and Luke not specifying the day. As Jesus rode into Jerusalem the people there lay down their cloaks in front of him, and also lay down small branches of trees and sang part of Psalm 118: 25–26.

In the three synoptic gospels, entry into Jerusalem is followed by the Cleansing of the Temple episode, in which Jesus expels the money changers from the Temple, accusing them of turning the Temple to a den of thieves through their commercial activities. This is the only account of Jesus using physical force in any of the gospels. John 2:13-16 includes a similar narrative much earlier, and scholars debate if these refer to the same episode. The synoptics include a number of well known parables and sermons such as the Widow's mite and the Second Coming Prophecy during the week that follows.

In that week, the synoptics also narrate conflicts between Jesus and the elders of the Jews, in episodes such as the Authority of Jesus Questioned and the Woes of the Pharisees in which Jesus criticizes their hypocrisy. Judas Iscariot, one of the twelve apostles approaches the Jewish elders and performs the "Bargain of Judas" in which he accepts to betray Jesus and hand him over to the elders. Matthew specifies the price as thirty silver coins.

Last Supper

Jesus with the Eucharist (detail), by Juan de Juanes, mid-late 16th century.

In the New Testament, the Last Supper is the final meal that Jesus shares with his twelve apostles in Jerusalem before his crucifixion. The Last Supper is mentioned in all four canonical gospels, and Paul's First Epistle to the Corinthians (11:23-26), which was likely written before the gospels, also refers to it.

In all four gospels, during the meal, Jesus predicts that one of his Apostles will betray him. Jesus is described as reiterating, despite each Apostle's assertion that he would not betray Jesus, that the betrayer would be one of those who were present. In Matthew 26:23–25 and John 13:26–27 Judas is specifically singled out as the traitor.

In Matthew 26:26–29, Mark 14:22–25, Luke 22:19–20 Jesus takes bread, breaks it and gives it to the disciples, saying: "This is my body which is given for you". Although the Gospel of John does not include a description of the bread and wine ritual during the Last Supper, most scholars agree that John 6:58–59 (the Bread of Life Discourse) has a Eucharistic nature and resonates with the "words of institution" used in the synoptic gospels and the Pauline writings on the Last Supper.

In all four gospels Jesus predicts that Peter will deny knowledge of him, stating that Peter will disown him three times before the rooster crows the next morning. The synoptics mention that after the arrest of Jesus Peter denied knowing him three times, but after the third denial, heard the rooster crow and recalled the prediction as Jesus turned to look at him. Peter then began to cry bitterly.

The Gospel of John provides the only account of Jesus washing his disciples' feet before the meal. John's Gospel also includes a long sermon by Jesus, preparing his disciples (now without Judas) for his departure.

Chapters 14–17 of the Gospel of John are known as the *Farewell discourse* given by Jesus, and are a rich source of Christological content.

Agony in the Garden, betrayal and arrest

Main articles: Agony in the Garden, Kiss of Judas, and Arrest of Jesus

See also: Holy Hour

In Matthew 26:36–46, Mark 14:32–42, Luke 22:39–46 and John 18:1, immediately after the Last Supper, Jesus takes a walk to pray, Matthew and Mark identifying this place of prayer as Garden of Gethsemane.

While in the Garden, Judas appears, accompanied by a crowd that includes the Jewish priests and elders and people with weapons. Judas gives Jesus a kiss to identify him to the crowd who then arrests Jesus. One of Jesus' disciples tries to stop them and uses a sword to cut off the ear of one of the men in the crowd. Luke states that Jesus miraculously healed the wound and John and Matthew state that Jesus criticized the violent act, insisting that his disciples should not resist his arrest. In Matthew 26:52 Jesus makes the well known statement: *all who live by the sword, shall die by the sword*.

Prior to the arrest, in Matthew 26:31 Jesus tells the disciples: "All ye shall be offended in me this night" and in 32 that: "But after I am raised up, I will go before you into Galilee." After his arrest, Jesus' disciples go into hiding.

Trials by the Sanhedrin, Herod and Pilate

Main articles: Sanhedrin trial of Jesus, Pilate's Court, Jesus at Herod's Court, *and* Crown of Thorns

See also: Jesus, King of the Jews *and* What is truth?

In the narrative of the four canonical gospels after the betrayal and arrest of Jesus, he is taken to the Sanhedrin, a Jewish judicial body. Jesus is tried by the Sanhedrin, mocked and beaten and is condemned for making claims of being the Son of God. He is then taken to Pontius Pilate and the Jewish elders ask Pilate to judge and condemn Jesus—accusing him of claiming to be the King of the Jews. After questioning, with few replies provided by Jesus, Pilate publicly declares that he finds Jesus innocent, but the crowd insists on punishment. Pilate then orders Jesus' crucifixion. Although the gospel accounts vary with respect to various details, they agree on the general character and overall structure of the trials of Jesus.

Jesus in the upper right hand corner, his hands bound behind, is being tried at the high priest's house and turns to look at Peter, in Rembrandt's 1660 depiction of Peter's denial.

In, Matthew 26:57, Mark 14:53 and Luke 22:54 Jesus was taken to the high priest's house where he was mocked and beaten that night. The next day, early in the morning, the chief priests and scribes lead Jesus away into their council. In John 18:12–14, however, Jesus is first taken to Annas, the father-in-law of Caiaphas, and then to Caiaphas. All four gospels include the *Denial of Peter* narrative, where Peter denies knowing Jesus three times, at which point the rooster crows as predicted by Jesus.

In the gospel accounts Jesus speaks very little, mounts no defense and gives very infrequent and indirect answers to the questions of the priests, prompting an officer to slap him. In Matthew 26:62 the lack of response from Jesus prompts the high priest to ask him: "Answerest thou nothing?" In Mark 14:61 the high priest then asked Jesus: "Are you the Christ, the Son of the Blessed?" And Jesus said, "I am" — at which point the high priest tore his own robe in anger and accused Jesus of blasphemy. In Luke 22:70 when asked: "Are you then the Son of God?" Jesus answers: "You say that I am" affirming the title Son of God.

Taking Jesus to Pilate's Court, the Jewish elders ask Pontius Pilate to judge and condemn Jesus—accusing him of claiming to be the King of the Jews. In Luke 23:7–15 Pilate realizes that Jesus is a Galilean, and is thus under the jurisdiction of Herod Antipas. Pilate sends Jesus to Herod to be tried. However, Jesus says almost nothing in response to Herod's questions. Herod and his soldiers mock Jesus, put a gorgeous robe on him, as the King of the Jews, and sent him back to Pilate. Pilate then calls together the Jewish elders, and says that he has "found no fault in this man."

The use of the term king is central in the discussion between Jesus and Pilate. In John 18:36 Jesus states: "My kingdom is not of this world", but does not directly deny being the King of the Jews. Pilate then writes "Jesus of Nazareth, King of the Jews" as a sign (abbreviated as INRI in depictions) to be affixed to the cross of Jesus.

The trial by Pilate is followed by the flagellation episode, the soldiers mock Jesus as the King of Jews by putting a purple robe (that signifies royal status) on him, place a Crown of Thorns on his head, and beat and mistreat him in Matthew 27:29–30, Mark 15:17–19 and John 19:2–3. Jesus is then sent to Calvary for crucifixion.

Crucifixion and burial

Pietro Perugino's depiction of the Crucifixion as *Stabat Mater*, 1482.

Jesus' crucifixion is described in all four canonical gospels, and is attested to by other sources of that age (e.g. Josephus and Tacitus), and is regarded as an historical event.

After the trials, Jesus made his way to Calvary (the path is traditionally called via Dolorosa) and the three synoptic gospels indicate that he was assisted by Simon of Cyrene, the Romans compelling him to do so. In Luke 23:27–28 Jesus tells the women in the multitude of people following him not to cry for him but for themselves and their children. Once at Calvary (Golgotha), Jesus was offered wine mixed with gall to drink — usually offered as a form of painkiller. Matthew's and Mark's gospels state that he refused this.

The soldiers then crucified Jesus and cast lots for his clothes. Above Jesus' head on the cross was the inscription King of the Jews, and the soldiers and those passing by mocked him about the title. Jesus was crucified between two convicted thieves, one of whom rebuked Jesus, while the other defended him. Each gospel has its own account of Jesus' last words, comprising the seven last sayings on the cross. In John 19:26–27 Jesus entrusts his mother to the disciple he loved and in Luke 23:34 he states: "Father, forgive them; for they know not what they do", usually interpreted as his forgiveness of the Roman soldiers and the others involved.

The Roman soldiers did not break Jesus' legs, as they did to the other two men crucified (breaking the legs hastened the crucifixion process), as Jesus was dead already. One of the soldiers traditionally known as Saint Longinus, pierced the side of Jesus with a lance and water flowed out. In Mark 15:39, impressed by the events the Roman centurion calls Jesus the Son of God.

Following Jesus' death on Friday, Joseph of Arimathea asked the permission of Pilate to remove the body. The body was removed from the cross, was wrapped in a clean cloth and buried in a new rock-hewn tomb, with the assistance of Nicodemus. In Matthew 27:62–66 the Jews go to Pilate the day after the crucifixion and ask for guards for the tomb and also seal the tomb with a stone as well as the guard, to be sure the body remains there.

Resurrection and ascension

The New Testament accounts of the resurrection and ascension of Jesus, state that the first day of the week after the crucifixion (typically interpreted as a Sunday), his followers encounter him risen from the dead, after his tomb is discovered to be empty. The resurrected Jesus appears to them that day and a number of times thereafter, delivers sermons and commissions them, before ascending to Heaven. Two of the canonical gospels (Luke and Mark) include a brief mention of the Ascension, but the main references to it are elsewhere in the New Testament.

In the four canonical gospels, when the tomb of Jesus is discovered empty, in Matthew 28:5, Mark 16:5, Luke 24:4 and John 20:12 his resurrection is announced and explained to the followers who arrive there early in the morning by either one or two beings (either men or angels) dressed in bright robes who appear in or near the tomb. Mark 16:9 and John 20:15 indicate that Jesus appeared to the Magdalene first, and Luke 16:9 states that she was among the Myrrh bearers.

After the discovery of the empty tomb, the gospels indicate that Jesus made a series of appearances to the disciples. These include the well known Doubting Thomas episode and the Road to Emmaus appearance where Jesus meets two disciples. The catch of 153 fish appearance includes a miracle at the Sea of Galilee, and thereafter Jesus encourages Peter to serve his followers. The final post-resurrection appearance in the gospel accounts is when Jesus ascends to Heaven. Luke 24:51 states that Jesus "was carried up into heaven". The ascension account is elaborated in Acts 1:1–11 and mentioned 1 Timothy 3:16. In Acts 1:1–9, forty days after the resurrection, as the disciples look on, "he was taken up; and a cloud received him out of their sight." 1 Peter 3:22 describes Jesus as being on "the right hand of God, having gone into heaven".

The Acts of the Apostles also contain "post-ascension" appearances by Jesus. These include the vision by Stephen just before his death in Acts 7:55, and the road to Damascus episode in which Apostle Paul is converted to Christianity. The instruction given to Ananias in Damascus in Acts 9:10–18 to heal Paul is the last reported conversation with Jesus in the Bible until the Book of Revelation was written.

Appendix II –

Example Template for your Testimony

1. Who do you go to, to get your strength?
2. Who is the enemy (your enemy)?
3. What gives you daily strength?
4. Who are the other teammates on your team?
5. What shield of protection are you putting on each day (What suit are you wearing)?
6. Is your suit always on or do you hide yourself – by taking your suit off??   Do you hide your light away? Do you allow others to see your light?
7. Brainstorm about yourself (after your Spiritual Birth in Christ – as a Christian)
8. Write out your testimony.
9. Who were you before?
10. How were you found?
11. Where were you when that someone reached out to you?

Start Your Testimony here with all the details that you have gathered from the questions above.

_____

_____

_____

_____

_____

_____

_____

_____

_____

_____

_____

_____

_____

_____

_____

_____

_____

Citation

1. "Jesus", last modified October 25, 2022, https://en.wikipedia.org/wiki/Jesus.

2. "Moses", last modified October 26, 2022, https://en.wikipedia.org/wiki/Moses.

3. "Daniel (biblical figure), last modified October 9, 2022, https://en.wikipedia.org/wiki/Daniel_(biblical_figure).

4. "Paul the Apostle", last modified October 26, 2022, https://en.wikipedia.org/wiki/Paul_the_Apostle.

5. "Joseph (Genesis)", last modified October 20, 2022, https://en.wikipedia.org/wiki/Joseph_(Genesis).

6. "David", last modified October 26, 2022, https://en.wikipedia.org/wiki/David.

7. "Spider-man", last modified October 26, 2022, https://en.wikipedia.org/wiki/Spider-Man.

8. "Hulk", last modified October 26, 2022, https://en.wikipedia.org/wiki/Hulk.

9. "Wolverine", last modified October 9, 2022, https://en.wikipedia.org/wiki/Wolverine_(character).

10. "Superman", last modified October 26, 2022, https://en.wikipedia.org/wiki/Superman.

11. "Wonder Woman", last modified October 22, 2022, https://en.wikipedia.org/wiki/Wonder_Woman.

12. What Happened To The 12 Disciples? Last modified February 11, 2020, https://www.faithonhill.com/blog/what-happened-to-the-12-disciples.

Appendix III –

Additional Scriptures Revealing God's Power

Judges 6:34 (NLT)

Then the Spirit of the Lord clothed Gideon with power. He blew a ram's horn as a call to arms, and the men of the clan of Abiezer came to him.

Judges 14:6 (NLT)

At that moment the Spirit of the Lord came powerfully upon him, and he ripped the lion's jaws apart with his bare hands. He did it as easily as if it were a young goat. But he didn't tell his father or mother about it.

Judges 14:19 (NLT)

Then the Spirit of the Lord came powerfully upon him. He went down to the town of Ashkelon, killed thirty men, took their belongings, and gave their clothing to the men who had solved his riddle. But Samson was furious about what had happened, and he went back home to live with his father and mother.

Judges 15:14 (NLT)

As Samson arrived at Lehi, the Philistines came shouting in triumph. But the Spirit of the Lord came powerfully upon Samson, and he snapped the ropes on his arms as if they were burnt strands of flax, and they fell from his wrists.

Judges 16:24 (NLT)

When the people saw him, they praised their god, saying, "Our god has delivered our enemy to us! The one who killed so many of us is now in our power!"

1 Samuel 2:10 (NLT)

Those who fight against the Lord will be shattered. He thunders against them from heaven; the Lord judges throughout the earth. He gives power to his king; he increases the strength of his anointed one."

1 Samuel 7:13 (NLT)

So the Philistines were subdued and didn't invade Israel again for some time. And throughout Samuel's lifetime, the Lord's powerful hand was raised against the Philistines.

1 Samuel 10:6 (NLT)

At that time the Spirit of the Lord will come powerfully upon you, and you will prophesy with them. You will be changed into a different person.

1 Samuel 10:10 (NLT)

When Saul and his servant arrived at Gibeah, they saw a group of prophets coming toward them. Then the Spirit of God came powerfully upon Saul, and he, too, began to prophesy.

1 Samuel 11:6 (NLT)

Then the Spirit of God came powerfully upon Saul, and he became very angry.

1 Samuel 16:13 (NLT)

So as David stood there among his brothers, Samuel took the flask of olive oil he had brought and anointed David with the oil. And the Spirit of the Lord came powerfully upon David from that day on. Then Samuel returned to Ramah.

1 Samuel 24:15 (NLT)

May the Lord therefore judge which of us is right and punish the guilty one. He is my advocate, and he will rescue me from your power!"

2 Samuel 22:3 (NLT)

my God is my rock, in whom I find protection. He is my shield, the power that saves me, and my place of safety. He is my refuge, my savior, the one who saves me from violence.

2 Samuel 22:18 (NLT)

He rescued me from my powerful enemies, from those who hated me and were too strong for me.

2 Kings 17:36 (NLT)

But worship only the Lord, who brought you out of Egypt with great strength and a powerful arm. Bow down to him alone, and offer sacrifices only to him.

Isaiah 63:12 (NLT)

Where is the one whose power was displayed when Moses lifted up his hand— the one who divided the sea before them, making himself famous forever?

Jeremiah 32:21 (NLT)

"You brought Israel out of Egypt with mighty signs and wonders, with a strong hand and powerful arm, and with overwhelming terror.

Hosea 1:7 (NLT)

But I will show love to the people of Judah. I will free them from their enemies—not with weapons and armies or horses and charioteers, but by my power as the Lord their God."

Amos 5:9 (NLT)

With blinding speed and power he destroys the strong, crushing all their defenses.

Jonah 1:4 (NLT)

But the Lord hurled a powerful wind over the sea, causing a violent storm that threatened to break the ship apart.

Jonah 1:16 (NLT)

The sailors were awestruck by the Lord's great power, and they offered him a sacrifice and vowed to serve him.

Micah 3:8 (NLT)

But as for me, I am filled with power— with the Spirit of the Lord. I am filled with justice and strength to boldly declare Israel's sin and rebellion.

Micah 4:8 (NLT)

As for you, Jerusalem, the citadel of God's people, your royal might and power will come back to you again. The kingship will be restored to my precious Jerusalem.

Nahum 1:3 (NLT)

The Lord is slow to get angry, but his power is great, and he never lets the guilty go unpunished. He displays his power in the whirlwind and the storm. The billowing clouds are the dust beneath his feet.

Habakkuk 3:4 (NLT)

His coming is as brilliant as the sunrise. Rays of light flash from his hands, where his awesome power is hidden.

Haggai 2:22 (NLT)

I will overthrow royal thrones and destroy the power of foreign kingdoms. I will overturn their chariots and riders. The horses will fall, and their riders will kill each other.

Matthew 1:18 (NLT)

The Birth of Jesus the Messiah

This is how Jesus the Messiah was born. His mother, Mary, was engaged to be married to Joseph. But before the marriage took place, while she was still a virgin, she became pregnant through the power of the Holy Spirit.

Printed in the USA
CPSIA information can be obtained
at www.ICGtesting.com
CBHW061913300724
12440CB00019B/349